Developing Feature Films in Europe

Developing Feature Films in Europe

A practical guide

Angus Finney

a BLUEPRINT book
published by Routledge

London and New York

First published 1996
by Routledge
11 New Fetter Lane, London EC4P 4EE

Simultaneously published in the USA and Canada
by Routledge
29 West 35th Street, New York, NY 10001

© 1996 Angus Finney

Typeset in Palatino by WestKey Ltd., Falmouth, Cornwall
Printed and bound in Great Britain by
TJ Press (Padstow) Ltd, Padstow, Cornwall

British Library Cataloguing in Publication Data
A catalogue record for this book is available from the British Library

Library of Congress Cataloguing in Publication Data
A catalogue record for this book is available from the Library of Congress

ISBN 0–415–13661–X

Dedicated to Tiernan MacBride, for his generous support to Europe's film industry. RIP.

Contents

Preface

The current crisis in the European film industry could be summed up by the fact that over the last two decades, European films have suffered a progressive loss of their own theatrical market and two-thirds of the cinema-going audience.

In most European countries, American-produced films are attracting more than 80% of the cinema box-office revenues – in some countries this figure exceeds 90% – and 40% of Europe's television audience ratings. Only 20% of European films are shown in territories beyond their national borders and very few of these films are distributed successfully throughout Europe. Overall, European-produced films have been increasingly restricted to their domestic markets.

The highly realistic scenario outlined above explains the measures of support that the European Commission has been providing for the European audiovisual industry, including the 1991–1995 MEDIA Programme in general, and the Media Business School (MBS) in particular.

Three key elements are needed for the development of a strong European film industry. They include the need to create a market for products, the production of films aimed for that market and the development of a training scheme for professionals. Or, what would amount to the same thing, concerted action in the development and distribution of audiovisual products and training in business skills. The three concepts apply to the major policy themes currently under consideration in the EU and represent the three main areas in which the new MEDIA Programme, announced as MEDIA 2, will take action in the future.

These three areas are not isolated factors – they call for horizontal coordination. Action in training should focus on projects worthy and capable of being developed and produced for a strong market.

At the MBS we believe the pivotal point lies in *research* and the access to factual data connected with the market. European producers need a better knowledge and understanding of the market which they can only achieve through professional training supported by research and a publications policy. This scheme, which also has a direct bearing on development and distribution, has been a crucial part of the work at the MBS over the last 5 years and has proved to be a key element in the development of actions capable of addressing the *priority* elements to be dealt with in the new EU action plan.

Developing Feature Films in Europe – A Practical Guide is being published with a view to emphasizing the role of development within the overall process of film-making. Strong development is crucial if our films are to reach a wider European and international audience. The book is the first in-depth examination of current European development practices and we hope will highlight for professionals the potential improvements in this key area.

I would like to thank the author, Angus Finney, for his meticulous work, and also all those professionals who have lent their opinions and numerous experiences to making this new publication on the European audiovisual industry possible.

Fernando Labrada
MBS General Manager

Acknowledgements

The methodology behind the research project upon which this MBS publication is based was as follows: in order to cover Europe as a whole, a team of professional researchers was established by the author. Reports of their research into development formed a considerable bank of material for this publication.

The research team for this publication was: Martin Blaney (Germany), Margaret Dolley (Norway and Denmark), Anna Franklin (Eastern Europe), Patrick Frater (France), Linda Moore (Spain), Alois Razoumeenko (Iceland), Ruppert Widdicombe and Anneli Bojstad (Portugal), Deborah Wolfson (UK), and Deborah Young (Italy). Additional research support was carried out by Amanda Harrison, Trine Piil and Helena Murrell (MBS).

In addition to the above, a wide range of industry professionals helped the author and the MBS research team to execute this work. The author is grateful to the 70 or so individuals who donated significant time to assist this book. They include: Maurizio Amati, David Aukin, Chris Auty, Dr Andrew Barry, Henrik Bering Liisberg, Didier Boujard, Stephen Bradley, Deborah Burton, Gabriella Carosio, Giuseppe Cereda, René Cleitman, Dinah Costes-Brook, Pippa Cross, Bo Christensen, Noëlle Deschamps, Sean Dromgoole, Mads Egmont, Bernd Eichinger, Eric Fellner, James Flynn, Bengt Forslund, Julian Friedmann, Dieter Geissler, Ben Gibson, Renée Goddard, Johnny Gogan, Andrés Vicente Gómez, Ed Guiney, Peter Hald, Brook Hoadley, Jan Erik Holst, Phil Hughes, Klaus Keil, Albert Kitzler, Lars Kolvig, Jack Lechner, Pekka Lehto, Eugenia Liroudia, Claudia Longerich, Ivan McTaggart, Lynda Myles, Simon Perry, Gabriela Pfandner, Mick Pilsworth, Joaquim Pinto, Erwin Provoost, David Puttnam, Raymond Ravar, Simon Relph, Ryclef Rienstra, Christian Routh, Claudine Sainderichin, Antonio Saura, Gerhard Schmidt, Mark Shivas, Bernie Stampfer, Manuela Stehr, Nicolas Steil, Rod Stoneman, Karen Street, Lasse Svanberg, Istvan Szabo, Stewart Till, Gilles-Marie Tine, Neil Watson, Dick Willemsen, Stephen Woolley, Colin Young and Krzyzstof Zanussi.

Lastly, I would like to thank my editors at the MBS, Isabel de las Casas and Nadine Luque, who have supported the project and provided helpful suggestions and encouragement at all times.

Angus Finney

An introduction to feature film development

1

The level of awareness about the strategic role of development across much of the European film industry has risen in the last 5 years. The Media Business School (MBS) research upon which this book is based examined national and pan-European funds, the private sector, broadcasters, and certain training initiatives. The results of that research indicated that public funds such as the European Script Fund (SCRIPT), alongside initiatives implemented by the MBS such as ACE – Ateliers du Cinéma Européen and PILOTS (the Programme for the International Launch of Television Series), have helped change the perception that development was merely an irritating starting block, while the main business of films was to be found in the production process.

The political environment has also moved forward. In the 1994 European Commission's Green Paper on Audiovisual Policy a diagnosis of the structural shortcomings of the European programme industry argued that: 'At the creation stage, European projects are handicapped by a lack of development. This is the crucial stage where original ideas must be reworked and geared towards wider audiences'.

The diagnosis went on to argue that it was 'regrettable that some public support mechanisms are unduly restricted to domestic production and do not give sufficient incentive to work for European and transnational markets. This creative/development stage is essential: even with the most sophisticated distribution mechanisms, if no account is taken of the audience's tastes and demands, the European film industry will never be competitive'.

Hence, support for development activity was underlined as a priority sector for the future building of the European audiovisual industry.

1.1 THE WIDER PERSPECTIVE

Europe currently has an annual audiovisual trade deficit of more than $3.7 billion with North America. US-produced films and programmes are currently taking around 80% of Europe's cinema box-office revenues and 40% of Europe's television audience ratings.

Among the different approaches and cost structures of the different industries, there is one area where the US spends significantly more than Europe: development. Around 7% of the US's total audiovisual revenue, and up to 10% of each film's budget, is invested on development. In stark contrast, Europe tends to spend a much lower percentage, estimated at between 1 and 2% of each film budget.

1.2   DEFINING THE ACTIVITY OF DEVELOPMENT

Development is the chronological starting point for all producers, writers and most directors when entering the film industry. It is the place from where ideas should be stimulated and encouraged to grow, and where initial deals are made. As such, it is a fundamental bedrock to subsequent film activities such as production, distribution and marketing.

For the purposes of this book, the activity is defined as the work surrounding the initial screenwriting process, the raising of finance and the initial planning of production. In addition to the writing of treatments and full screenplay drafts, development activity includes the time and money spent in building a project, attracting talent and the marketing of a concept to potential financiers. It is not normally seen as part of the pre-production process where locations, casting and line budgets are prepared. However, in certain cases scripts are further developed, perhaps because of casting or director's requirements.

1.3   THE EARLY STAGES OF DEVELOPMENT

The initial idea stage is a loosely structured area with a considerable number of possibilities. An idea may take a variety of routes towards a full script commission. The flow chart in Figure 1 shows some of the different routes that can be taken.

The initial idea of a script [1] can be an idea, treatment or first-draft script. Unsolicited scripts from unknown writers [2] will in the majority of instances move through to a reader first [3]. Most of them will be rejected. A very small percentage will come through as an idea [1] from development. Ideas also come from contacts [4]; a pitch by [5] or commission to [6] a known/established screenplay writer; or from the buying of a book option [7]. A large number of producers also generate ideas themselves [8].

The producer will then assess [9] the basic idea. On this basis the producer may decide to go ahead with development, or to drop the project [10]. However, the originator of an idea may have benefited from the contact, even if the idea did not make it any further.

To develop an idea, a producer will need to secure finance [12]. This can

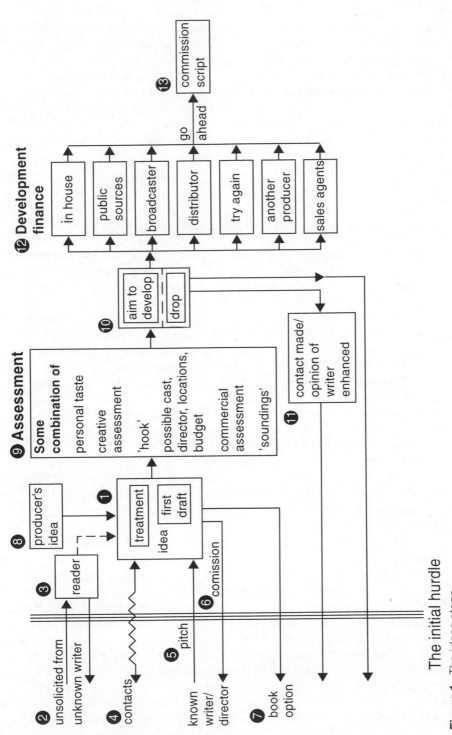

Figure 1 The ideas stage
Source: NFTS

The initial hurdle

⑨ Assessment

Some combination of

personal taste

creative assessment

'hook'

possible cast, director, locations, budget

commercial assessment

'soundings'

⑫ Development finance

in house

public sources

broadcaster

distributor

try again

another producer

sales agents

go ahead

⑬ commission script

⑩ aim to develop / drop

⑪ contact made/ opinion of writer enhanced

⑧ producer's idea

① treatment / first draft

idea

⑥ comission

③ reader

② unsolicited from unknown writer

④ contacts

⑤ pitch

known writer/ director

⑦ book option

come from an in-house source, from a public development fund, a broadcaster, a sales agent, a distributor or a private investor. However, the last three sources are often rare in the European film industry.

The producer also has to make a commitment in terms of time and planning, often incurring considerable expense through travelling to potential financiers, markets and festivals. They will have to put a development budget together at this stage. In addition, another producer or potential co-financier may help with development finance. Once the finance structure has been at least part-raised, the idea will move into a fully-fledged development stage. This normally includes a first draft, two re-writes [13] and the active raising of finance around the growing package.

1.4 DEVELOPMENT AS A HIGH-RISK INVESTMENT

Figure 1 may give the impression that there is a straightforward, typical standard for developing ideas. However, the truth is that feature film development is an inexact science. While there are many ways to move a project toward production, one element remains consistent throughout Europe: development is a high-risk stage of film production. There are no guarantees of a project's successful journey from idea through to treatment and drafts, from screenplay to production, on to distribution and exhibition, and to what should be the ultimate goal: an audience.

It is also a relatively expensive area of risk investment. For example, a European film with a budget of ECU 2–3m may cost between ECU 50 000 and 150 000 minimum to develop. Large-budget films by European standards of around ECU 8–10m may cost as much as ECU 250 000 to move through development and into production.

A decade ago, the development process within Europe's film industry was a poorly defined, secondary element to the notion of entering film production. Indeed, most practitioners would have assumed that development had something to do with scripts, and left it at that. Scripts, and the writing of them – albeit not necessarily the development of them in the fuller sense of the activity – became the focal point for the early stages of film production.

The surrounding but strategically central elements to the script itself tended to be side-stepped or simply not recognized. These include research and acquisitions of rights for source material, treatment development, the raising of finance, the marketing of the package, the attachment of talent and the costs of paying script editors or hiring additional writers.

Historically, the European producer has traditionally looked at the development costs against the projected return from fees and retained rights. The preoccupation with production has partly stemmed from the fact that when producers are in production, they are being paid. This approach has tended to obscure the financial and practical elements essential to a healthy development process. It has also led the producer to take a less realistic view of the projected 'value' of a project and how to realize that value in the marketplace.

1.5 THE 'AUTEUR' PROBLEM

Part of Europe's problem regarding development is an historical one and stems from a very strongly developed 'auteur' culture, where film directors have enjoyed most of the power in the film-making process. The results of this dependence have led to feature films tending to be rescued in the cutting room by film editors rather than script editors before the main money was ever spent. European writers have tended to be marginalized by the auteur system, while producers also lost out and have been traditionally seen as financial servants for directors. Most experienced writers, script editors and agents suggested to the author that Europe's producers are often underskilled when it comes to script reading and editing.

For further evidence, it is instructive to turn to the findings of the MBS research. The majority of film producers interviewed for the MBS study were astonishingly vague about their levels of development spending and strategy. Producers replied to the direct questions asked in one or more of the following ways:

1. They did not know how much they spend on development per year.
2. They had no idea what they were spending on development 5 years ago.
3. They could normally only estimate how much they had spent on each individual project.

1.6 EUROPE'S DIFFERENT APPROACHES

Significantly different attitudes toward and understanding of development were apparent from territory to territory, and region to region. At their most basic, it was clear that the UK and Ireland have been influenced to an extent by a largely shared language and links with North America. As a consequence the UK has, at first glance, a fairly advanced notion of what development means. Writers' agents also play a major role in the development process in English-speaking territories (see Chapter 2).

France has been heavily influenced by the director-led, 'auteur' approach. Experienced writers are much more rare than directors who also write their own scripts. And producers tend to concentrate on tapping a subsidy system that tends to reward film-makers when actually in production, and not at the development stage.

Germany has an extensive script-support system in its regional public subsidy network. However, this has tended to be limited to the production of scripts, rather than the fully-fledged development of projects intended for an audience. The result has been a high number of scripts written, but significantly fewer produced at a standard that has attracted audiences in Germany, let alone across Europe or the rest of the world.

Most significantly, southern European territories share a distinctly less conscious notion of feature film development. This is due to a combination of factors. Italy and, to a lesser extent, Spain have been heavily influenced by 'auteur' trends. Screenplay writers (and editors) are not regarded as essential to the film-making process, with directors normally assumed to be the writers in most cases. The Italian subsidy system offers no financial support at the development stage, while Spain has only recently begun to consider development support, and even that is in relatively small amounts.

1.7   THE HOLLYWOOD APPROACH

How does the situation in Europe compare to that in Hollywood? Any comprehensive notions of a fully-fledged, integrated development process were, and still are, generally found within the Hollywood studio system, as opposed to Europe's far more fragmented film environment. Europe's independent film-makers lack Hollywood-type studio infrastructures. They rarely have the capital with which to invest in development. Individually run companies are forced to drive their ideas and scripts up from the bottom, and the potential for a national film producer to recoup the costs of a production from that territory alone are almost impossible. Europe's domestic markets are simply not large enough to recoup costs.

'On-the-block' development deals – where a production company is attached to a studio – hardly exist in Europe, mainly because there are no studios operating on the same scale as in Hollywood. The exceptions include PolyGram Filmed Entertainment, Chargeurs, Sogepaq and CiBy 2000, but across the continent they are virtually extinct.

A major studio or film production company with a regular output of films tends to view development as a fixed cost within its overall business plan. A portion of this expenditure is allocated to each film as an above-the-line cost. In Hollywood, the development costs are placed at around 8–10% of a film's total budget. Hollywood's development:production success ratio is very low, with only around one in 20 projects finally reaching production. As ACE Director Colin Young points out: 'A huge number of films are put into development in the US, but they never actually reach production. This system is considered fine by the major Hollywood studios and is clearly one reason that explains the studios' huge overhead cost of making a film'. Put simply, the successful films that go on to make a profit repay the costs of unmade scripts and projects. Profits are then pumped back into the development system, and the cycle of production is continued.

The US film industry's development budget was placed at around $500m a year by professionals. 'That is what Europe is competing with', explained producer David Puttnam. 'It is administered by very experienced executives working at an energy level almost unknown in Europe. It is fed by a very aggressive and well-run agency system at every level. The process is on a different planet'.

1.8 PRIVATE SOURCES OF DEVELOPMENT

Given the highly mature, industrial nature of the Hollywood studio system, it is understandable that the system attracts considerable levels of private investment. In contrast, the MBS research on European development underlined the structural weaknesses that continue to haunt the European film industry. Private development sources remain very hard to attract. The problem appears to lie not just in the levels of money available for investment, but in the incentives being offered. The risks involved in feature film development are very high, hence private financial investors expect to take stakes that are rewarded both from the production budget and from the eventual profits, if there are any, to be tapped.

Building assets and stronger companies is a clear answer to some of the problems of dependency discussed in this essay. This goes some way to explain the relatively new emphasis in Europe on public development support for companies in addition to writer and producer support.

1.9 MEDIA PROGRAMME'S INTERVENTION

Research for the MBS development study indicated that the link between development support and production investment through public film support mechanisms is starting to change.

Of the various elements of the European Commission's MEDIA Programme, the one which sought to act most directly on development was the European Script Fund (SCRIPT). SCRIPT has, through a variety of strategies, managed to adapt development from being merely an object of political rhetoric into something which can be effectively acted upon. Instead of seeing the idea of a development fund existing just for writers, SCRIPT was designed as a programme that would 'stimulate and encourage co-operative cross-border enterprise across the whole of Europe', according to founding Secretary-General Renée Goddard.

SCRIPT's specific action plan was launched in 1989 at a time when 'development' as a part of the production process was either unacknowledged or understood in radically different ways by European film administrators.

In this sense, SCRIPT's wider function has been to cast a spotlight on the whole development process behind a feature film's creation. SCRIPT has made development more concrete by helping its visibility. Rather than writers and producers only being recognized by financiers at the investment/production stage, their roles have been enhanced and revealed. SCRIPT has helped development become increasingly legitimate as a significant factor in the film production process. SCRIPT's activities have assisted film professionals to comprehend what 'development' can mean at a wide variety of levels and start to put it into practice.

KEY SUMMARY POINTS

1. Around 7% of the US's total audiovisual revenue, and up to 10% of each film's budget, is invested on development. In contrast, Europe tends to spend a much lower percentage, estimated at between 1 and 2%.
2. A decade ago, the development process within Europe's film industry was a poorly defined, secondary element to the notion of entering film production. Most practitioners would have assumed that development had something to do with scripts and left it at that.
3. Part of Europe's problem stems from a very strongly developed 'auteur' culture, where film directors have enjoyed the majority of the power in the film-making process.
4. Private development sources remain very hard to attract. The risks involved in feature film development are very high, hence private financial investors expect to take stakes that are rewarded both from the production budget and from the eventual profits, if there are any, to be tapped.
5. The European Script Fund has managed to adapt development into something which can be effectively acted upon. Instead of seeing the idea of a development fund existing just for writers, SCRIPT was designed as a programme that would 'stimulate and encourage co-operative cross-border enterprise across the whole of Europe'.

Creative aspects of film development

2

Many areas of this book examine public sources of development funding, along with private companies, independent producers and broadcasters, and their different approaches to development. However, the key starting point for every feature film is the 'idea'. The creative concept of what will make a potential film lies at the centre of development.

2.1 THE WRITER

The writer is at the heart of the creative development process. In many cases, they will either initiate an idea for an original screenplay, or suggest an adaptation of an existing book or other work. The writer may develop an outline of 1–2 pages, or a more fully-fledged treatment of 10–15 pages, before approaching a producer. More experienced writers are approached by producers to adapt their ideas for a film or to work on a story for which the producer owns the adaptation rights.

Few European screenwriters work in teams or even in pairs. This is a major contrast to Hollywood, where it is not unusual to find that a considerable number of writers have worked on a film screenplay. Many European screenwriters come from a television writing background, sometimes theatre, and often have written long-form literature such as novels and non-fiction books.

The majority of Europe's writers for cinema are isolated and unconnected from the main arteries of the film industry. Few are 'networked' into the channels that would help move their projects through development and into production. Above all, they often lack close and trusting relationships with film producers. Writers in Europe find it hard to find and develop the right links, productive introductions and stable conditions to work effectively.

The results of strong relationships are formidable. During the writing, development and production of Jean-Jacques Annaud's *The Name of the*

Rose, the writer and director of the complex production forged a highly productive relationship with its German producer, Bernd Eichinger. Together, they fought to raise the $30m budget and ultimately made one of the most successful European films ever made. 'I have never found that my producers are my enemies', explains French director Annaud. 'They are fighting for me, so I have to fight with them'.

Other professionals agree. For example, UK writer and director Terry Jones argues that a good producer can help the writer and the director have more freedom, not less. He also stresses teamwork, but warns that the relationship between the writer and the director has historically been difficult. 'Directors have treated writers very badly in the past, to the extent that some producers have had to go in and do something about it', says Jones, pointing out that during the 1970s many directors seemed to think that they were the only elements in a film that really mattered. 'Directing a film is much easier than writing it', he argues. 'The director is really answering a multiple-choice exam, while the writer is staring at a blank page every time he writes'.

2.2 THE DIFFERENT ROLES OF A PRODUCER

While the screenwriter is at the heart of the development process, the producer should be right there next to him or her. As American producer Art Linson pointed out in his book about producing in Hollywood (*A Pound of Flesh: Perilous Tales of How to Produce Movies in Hollywood*, Grove Press, 1993): 'What the movie is going to be about, and what the movie is going to be based on, are often decided by the producer. He must dream it up, have the first concept of what the picture should be when it is finished … The most significant contribution a producer makes to a movie occurs months, sometimes years, before the first day of filming'.

Producers often initiate films, raise the money for the rights to adapt them, hire the screenwriter(s) and, in certain cases, constructively analyse the scripts; but they neither write nor heavily re-write scripts. Ideas and, in certain cases, editing or re-structuring is one thing; fully-fledged writing is quite another. As Stephen Woolley, producer of Neil Jordan's *The Crying Game*, points out: 'One of the key jobs of the producer is to find ways of making the writer write better'.

The film industry tends to divide film producers into two rather vaguely defined camps: the **'creative'** producer and the **'financial'** producer. Few people are uniquely talented in both fields. Theoretically, an effective producing combination is one where two people – one creatively skilled and one financially inclined – work together on developing and producing projects. Often the term 'executive producer' is used for the producer who takes the lead role in the financial side of a project.

However, all film producers should know the details of the financial aspects of their project, 'creatively' inclined or not. And Europe does have certain individual producers who manage to combine these talents, including Claude Berri, Bernd Eichinger, Bo Christensen and Andrés Vicente Gómez, to name a few.

2.2.1 THE CREATIVE PRODUCER

One of the key functions of the creative producer is to develop a strong set of relationships with talent. Directors and actors are important, but the writer is where the development process starts. They normally build up a trust and an understanding over a considerable period of time. Whether it comes through story ideas, structural suggestions or simply an ability to help the writers keep improving their work, the producer needs to have the writer's respect and trust.

Creative producers read solicited and, in many cases, unsolicited story outlines of just a single page, 10–15-page treatments and scripts that are mostly in their first draft stage. These usually come to them either through writers, writer/director teams, talent agents or contacts and friends. In addition, producers have their own ideas and sources for potential screenplays. They read magazines and newspapers for ideas. A real news event might also provide an idea for a screenplay story. Musicals, songs, historic events, personal experience, old films or television plays and any other inspirational idea that might strike the producer are all valid starts in the development process. Above all, the producer needs to feel hugely enthusiastic about the idea. Unless a producer is deeply committed to an idea being realized as a feature film, how else is anybody going to support it?

The creative producer develops relationships with publishers, and attempts to see advance book lists and upcoming work as early as possible. If they think a book has potential for a screenplay, an option may be paid to the author of that work to reserve the right to adapt it for film. Normally, that payment is for a specific period, after which the option lapses and the screenplay rights revert to the author of the original work. Many producers take out a 2- or 3- year option on a work, and then renew that option if they feel there is a real chance of still putting the project into production.

The creative producer also develops strong relationships with writers, actors and directors' agents. Above all, it is their competence when dealing with talent that helps them develop successfully. Here, the balance between the producer and the director is important.

As Jean-Jacques Annaud points out: 'In Europe we say it's the director alone, in America they say it's the producer alone. The truth doesn't lie on one side or the other but in an harmonious mixture and understanding between the two. Most of the artistically and commercially successful movies ever made have been undertaken by a producer and a director who understood each other and have fought to make the movie for the same reasons'.

One of the key differences between Europe and Hollywood is the general absence of a fully integrated, developed agent system in Europe. With the relative exception of the UK, most European film-producing nations simply do not have agencies for screenwriting talent.

2.2.2   WORKING WITH AGENTS

Talent agents are a key part of the development process. From a writer's point of view, they normally charge a 10–15% commission on all sales of their work. The strength of agents is that they primarily have more information at their fingertips than most producers. For example, an agent will know about rival projects of a similar nature, the chances of putting strong combinations of actors together or a suitable director who is suddenly available. A good agent can encourage and lead the talent to the producer or vice versa, and consequently help a project raise its profile in the marketplace. Literary agents will sometimes discover a new talent or forward an interesting project to a producer.

Powerful Hollywood agencies have developed a reputation for aggressive '**packaging**', meaning – in Hollywood's terms – the pooling together of their key clients on one project and effectively keeping out the clients of other agents. However, there is a difference between 'packaging' and a well presented 'package' for any feature film or television project, which is essential to understand.

The word 'package' should not to be confused with the American concept of 'packaging', which was originally a US TV invention designed to maximize the commission made by agents for a product while minimizing the TV network's creative work and input. Actors, writers and directors belonging to the same agency were farmed out as a complete package, with no options offered to the broadcaster.

When this model was later adapted and aggressively applied by Hollywood super agency CAA it resulted in certain problems. The creative elements required to make up a film do not fit neatly into such streamlined, homogenized strategies. Packaging remains common in the US TV market, but less so in the feature film arena. Nevertheless, agents still heavily 'package' projects for the Hollywood studios.

However, in Europe, packaging has considerably less political and power-loaded connotations. An agent can help a producer create a strong combination of talent for a project. But the agent cannot make up for basic lack of knowledge. ICM UK agent Duncan Heath advises producers to make sure that they understand as much detail about the marketplace as possible, including the relative value of elements such as rights, an actor's worth in different territories or a director's bankability. 'The more knowledge you can build, the more power you have, and the less you (the producer) need to rely on an agent', he explains.

Some agents regard the early stages of development as a significant part of their jobs. 'I am usually the driving force behind taking a script into development, unless one of our writers already has a strong relationship with a producer', says Rochelle Stevens, a London-based literary agent. She stressed the importance of finding a producer to take a script on and the help an agent can provide in finding the right producer for the writer's project. Sometimes Stevens will work in tandem with a producer on a client's script, co-developing the project to a reasonably mature stage.

On the commercial side, good agents will also bear in mind what marketing elements the script will require to encourage investors to commit themselves. For example, if it is written by a first-time director, then perhaps it will need a 'named' or well known actor/actress for investors to feel more secure. Larger agencies are more powerful in this area, as they tend to send out their own writers' work to their signed-up acting and directing talent. On the other hand, if you are a young writer, then a large agency can be quite overwhelming, given their high work load and need to attend to their most famous (and demanding) clients. A less established writer is often better off going for a smaller, experienced agent who can nurture and develop his/her career.

2.2.3   THE HOLLYWOOD WAY

Overall, the Hollywood studio system offers an industrial approach towards development. Some typical scenarios are outlined below by German director Volker Schloendorff, who has worked both in Europe and Hollywood. He gives a very critical view of the development process inside the studios.

'A producer will meet with a studio executive and pitch an idea in around 10 minutes or so. The pitch needs to create enthusiasm if money for development is to be forthcoming. If the producer is not well known, but the studio executive likes the project, some $15 000–25 000 may be forwarded for further development. If the project is big, with a star already involved but not committed, the price can go up to $500 000 or much more, depending on the names of the writers and actors involved. From the first advance, the writer will be paid a first fee for writing a 'first draft', which is normally delivered in the first 3 months.

'The writer and the director talk about the project, which normally will not result in a first draft of the screenplay for 4 or 5 months. Both of them will be busy on other projects, slowing the process up'. Schloendorff points out that the 'hellish part' comes when the studios take on projects that they are not really committed to, but they have taken an option on in order to block that project being picked up and developed by another studio.

Projects are in 'development hell' for sometimes many months and then finally put into 'turnaround' – where the rights finally return to the producer. However, if another studio takes on the rights to that film, the original studio will demand its development costs back.

'If the first draft goes relatively well, and a star comes on board, a second draft is demanded. This often still needs work, so between three to five "re-writers" or "script doctors" are brought in for anything ranging from "polishes" – involving a few scenes and perhaps some fresh character dialogue – to complete re-writes. Often, the re-write has little in common with the original script, and it takes another writer to paste together the best of the original drafts. It is not an efficient system', Schloendorff concludes.

2.2.4   TAKING ON THE SCRIPT EDITORS

Others disagree, arguing that there are key elements in the studio approach that are very valuable at the development stage. The sheer level of investment in development – both in terms of time and money – is seen as a vital part of the industrial approach to film production. David Puttnam points out that the high levels of experience and energy invested in development 'are on a different planet' when compared with Europe. He argues that the Hollywood approach is about a 'demand-led industry, which is typified by identifying what the marketplace is seeking and where the gaps lie'.

Within the Hollywood system, there are key elements which help bind the development process together. For example, the role of the script editor is also an important aspect of creative development that Hollywood has embraced, a key function that European producers have tended to ignore. Editors are not employed on the Continent for feature film or television screenplay work. In the UK, script editors are more common, but they tend to be trained and employed only by television companies, and are often young and inexperienced, and aiming to fulfill that role only in order to move on to writing, directing or producing. Some literary and talent agents now employ trained script editors. For example, Sigrid Narjes, who runs Munich-based agency International Media Consulting, has hired an editor and argues that most writers are happy to work with one.

Good script editors, unlike most producers, can quickly spot structural holes in a screenplay. Problems with a screenplay can be solved far earlier with the help of an editor, saving a great deal of time and money later in the production and post-production process. 'A script that is far too long and ends up being shot is a disaster', warns German producer Bernd Eichinger. 'Of course, you can shoot it, and cut it in the editing room, but in the case of a big, $30m film, you are cutting away $10m that you could have saved in the first place'.

Although the MBS's PILOTS programme is not aimed at feature film screenwriters (see Appendix C for details), its 'training through the project' approach through the use of expert script editors, writers and agents (among others) has underlined certain key points. In addition to the value of editors, Julian Friedmann, PILOTS' head of studies, argues the following points:

- Visual stories have more impact than talking heads.
- People believe far more in what they see than in what they hear.
- Shorter scenes tend to be more involving.
- Over-written dialogue hinders material reaching wider audiences.
- A script editor can help the writer achieve more of the above.

However, while there are certain useful guidelines for development strategy, no two producers follow exactly the same paths. Two experienced British producers, David Puttnam and Jeremy Thomas, for example, go about development in substantially different ways.

Enigma, Puttnam's UK-based company, tends to find its own material to develop from books, topical news stories and so forth. Each project is then analysed as if it were a product. It is looked at from the point of view of the consumer – the audience – and adapted and changed. 'People hardly ever ask what the audience wants, who that likely audience is, and how are you going to reach it', explains Puttnam.

Writers are hired to develop the screenplays, under constant supervision from Puttnam's staff team, which includes trained script editors. The emphasis is on the project, rather than finding the right director at this stage of development. 'At Enigma we go through on average seven or eight drafts on a script. Sometimes we do much more', he says, pointing out that most scripts in Europe go through just two drafts before reaching the cameras.

In contrast, Jeremy Thomas's UK-based Recorded Picture Company only ever develops projects with a director attached. Managing director Chris Auty explains that, 'For us, the director is the beginning, middle and end of the equation. After all, why develop a script without knowing who will make your film? We don't buy a literary property and develop a script. Either a director has a pet project, or he comes to us and says that he wants to work with us. The central figure who is going to make the films is on board with us from the beginning'.

While Puttnam takes his development process through to eight or more drafts of a screenplay, Auty suggests that although there are no neat divisions, the strict development period of a project ends when the second screenplay draft is complete, and the initial approach for casting and location inspection are started. 'Of course, there's a gap between the completion of the screenplay and getting production finance in place, but the key is to bring all the elements – including the finance, cast, director and the completed screenplay – together at the same time'.

2.2.5   THE FINANCIAL PRODUCER

The 'financial' producer is the person responsible for bringing together the different elements of the film's budget. Like the creative producer they too are very aware of the 'value' of the project. That means they need to know how much the different 'elements' – including book option, writer, director, cast and genre – are worth in the marketplace. The financial producer should have box-office and sales figures on previous films made with all those elements; and details of previous similar genre pictures and their performances around the world. These are useful pitching tools for use in convincing people of the project's worth.

It is the financial producer who should know all the different international sales companies, key distributors in different territories, private banking sources, public subsidy funds and key executives in the medium and larger production companies around the world. They need to know how each institution works, but more importantly, who the key people are inside them. That includes knowing script readers and development executives, as well as top management. When a project is under consideration, every possible 'champion' inside a company or finance source can be vital.

Financial producers too will have opinions on the script, but in most cases it is the creative producer who helps the writing process develop on a day-to-day, week-by-week basis. Like the creative producer, financial producers do not write screenplays. Nor do they edit or re-write screenplays. They do frequently make useful suggestions. Normally these are filtered by the creative producer who picks up the good ones, and drops the less good ones.

Above all, it is the financial producer's task to take a project out into the market and 'test' it. That means finding out if the marketplace will support the making of the screenplay into a film. This may sound straightforward, but by the time that producer has approached the sales companies, distributors, banks and other sources of finance, he/she will have a strong impression about the project's potential to get made. All this work involves considerable time, travel and money.

It is also debatable at what stage sales agents and distributors should be approached in the development process. For example, Dieter Kosslick, the experienced German film administrator, suggests that it is better for the sales agents and distributors to be approached once a credible draft of the script has been prepared. Paris-based producer Jake Eberts agrees, arguing that just as the marketing departments in Hollywood should not interfere in a project's early development, neither should distributors in Europe. It is only later, once the project is properly presented, with many of the key elements (cast, director, budget, etc.) established, that the market can take a proper view of a project's full potential.

Lastly, many people involved in the MBS development research on which this book is based stressed that it is counter-productive to send an incomplete, unfinished, or early draft of a screenplay to potential backers. Most professionals only read a screenplay once. Most producers only have one bite of the cherry. Holding off until a screenplay is well developed can pay off heavily at a later stage in the development. It can make the difference between a project being financed or not.

KEY SUMMARY POINTS

1. The majority of Europe's writers for cinema are isolated and unconnected from the main arteries of the film industry. Few are 'networked' into the channels that would help move their projects through development and into production.
2. A key function of the 'creative' producer is to develop a strong set of relationships with talent. Directors and actors are important, but the writer is where the development process starts.
3. One of the key differences between Europe and Hollywood is the general absence of a fully integrated, developed agent system in Europe. With the relative exception of the UK, most European film-producing nations simply do not have agencies for talent.
4. The role of the script editor is an important aspect of creative development that Hollywood has embraced. This is a key function that European producers have tended to ignore. Editors are not employed on the Continent for feature film or television screenplay work.
5. Producers need to know how much the different 'elements', including book option, writer, director, cast, genre, etc., are worth in the marketplace. This information all stems from the initial script, upon which the package is built.

National public support systems for feature film development

3

3.1 INTRODUCTION TO THE NATIONAL SYSTEMS

Across much, but not all of Europe, there exists an extensive range of national public funding systems for feature film. Given that around 65% of the approximately 600 European films in production in mid-1995 were receiving public subsidies, the dependence on this source is clearly heavy. Most national funding systems were historically organized with the aim of supporting national production. The problem with this tendency is that many locally orientated systems fail to fit either co-production or co-financing models. Internal rules that have been designed to promote a national culture have tended to inhibit cross-border partnerships, a factor that applies to all European territories.

For example, in France, film production has been seen as a vehicle for sustaining both its language and culture. With these objectives firmly in mind, the government has long taken the view that films need to be supported. The preservation of local culture was also behind initial support in southern European countries like Spain, Portugal and Italy. However, in Italy, production support, let alone development support, has been dismantled over the last 3 years. In Germany, a grid of regional film support has been applied in a similar manner to the way local and national government has subsidized opera and theatre. Large amounts of public money has been invested in the regions to keep local arts operating. Without this support, regional theatre and opera would have died. See Figure 2 and Table 1.

However, the link between development support and production investment through public bodies is starting to change. Six or so years ago, the link was not always clear, with certain countries investing large sums in inexperienced scriptwriters, but few projects ever reaching production. The notion of development grants or loans for project packaging, script editing and marketing were unheard of.

No. of films

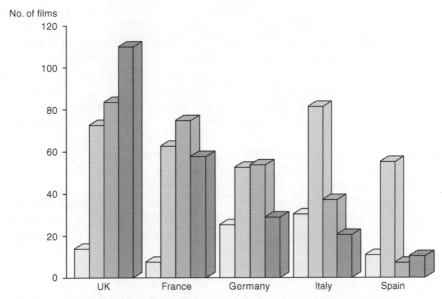

Figure 2 European films in development: ☐ less than $1m; ▨ $1–2.5m; ▨ $2.5–5m; ▨ more than $5m.

In contrast, new funds established since 1992/93 have tended to emphasize and expand the role of development. Instead of always thinking of the writer/director, funding bodies have started to think in stages of development loans. Initial monies are loaned to a writer. After a first draft is completed, a producer is encouraged to apply with that writer for further support. And the importance of further development funding for later script re-writing or project marketing is now embraced by many of Europe's larger national funding institutions.

Table 1 European films in development

Budget levels	UK	France	Germany	Italy	Spain
Below $1m	12	3	24	28	9
$1–2.5m	73	63	52	81	54
$2.5–5m	83	75	53	36	5
Above $5m	110	56	27	20	7
Total no. of films in development (1993)	493	260	193	187	96
Total no. of films in development (1994)	548	297	200	212	94

Source: European Film File/Screen International 1993/94.

These changes have in turn helped to alter the attitude of producers, many of whom have become increasingly committed to and involved in the wider development process. Instead of being able to apply for a one-off loan, they have had to return to the fund and have been asked to explain how the project is evolving before they can tap further support.

Beyond initial grants to single writers and writer-producer teams, many national funding systems are starting to consider supporting production companies over a longer period of time rather than just on a project-by-project basis. New adapted versions of the SCRIPT's Incentive Funding scheme – most notably, the CNC's 'Aide Au Développement' initiative (see France below) – are starting to spring up.

Territories that have modest to serious levels of national public support include Germany, France and the UK. However, France's support until recently has tended to be geared largely towards production investment, rather than development support. Territories that have very little or no development finance from public sources include Spain, Greece, Portugal and Italy. Smaller territories that do have some development support include Ireland, the Netherlands, Belgium, Scandinavia and Austria.

The following section examines the larger territories – including France, the UK, Germany, Italy and Spain, followed by a range of smaller territories (please note that practical information can be found in Appendix A at the back of the book).

3.2 FRANCE

Feature film production in France is only now beginning to emerge from under the shadow of the 'Nouvelle Vague'. In an auteur-dominated environment, feature film development was an idea in a director's head, rather than a team-driven process involving a serious input from a producer. Although the Nouvelle Vague was the genre through which directors such as Truffaut and Godard rose to international fame, it also led to imitators who were less able as writers and directors. However, these film-makers still justified their practice as being a personal view of the world, maintaining a tradition of the one-person, writer/director band with little regard for the audience.

Producers tended to become marginalized by the French 'auteur' system. Their skills were largely reduced to becoming financial servants for the all-powerful director. One of the main results of this trend was to breed producers who were invariably underskilled when it came to script commissioning, reading and editing. A perfunctory attitude towards pushing films quickly into production was predominant, with major implications for the relative health of French feature film development.

The above problems have been encouraged and exacerbated by the structure of subsidy support in France. The majority of the support is provided to film productions in such a way that it tends to reward film-makers when actually in production, but not at the development stage. This problem is discussed in the following examination of France's individual systems below.

Legal tendencies have also had a significant impact on film development and the respective roles of the writer/director versus the producer. French law asserts the primacy of the director through 'droit moral' ('moral right') over the copyright of the material. The consequences of the director's enhanced power has had problematic results. For example, scripts could be under-developed on the grounds that it was highly probable that film directors would change them during the shoot anyway.

Of the different French support systems, the **Centre National de la Cinématographie (CNC)** is the most important source of public funding in France and has some involvement with nearly every film produced in the country. It is currently re-directing its efforts toward producer and company-driven development and away from one-person writer/director support, as the details below suggest. Overall, state aid for the French film industry is extensive and complex in its application. However, monitoring of the industry and the high level of support granted to films is woefully low. According to Gilles-Marie Tine, former head of the CNC's selective subsidy department, there is no statistical information about the amount of development carried out in the French film industry.

This situation is not unusual across most states of the EU. It appears that national funding systems have tended – perhaps understandably – to invest the vast majority of their finances into productions and mechanisms, overlooking the need to record and compile information about their domestic industry. No Hollywood major studio would be incapable of knowing the statistical information about their development interests and investments over a 10-year period. Whether they choose to make it public is quite another matter.

It took a strong personality and famous film star to help shed some light on the French problem. Jeanne Moreau's recent honorary Presidency of the **'Avances Sur Recettes'** fund had a profound effect on the use of funding from France's leading selective subsidy pool. Until her tenure, the pool had mostly been used to fund production of first-time directors and second films. In a move later backed by Jacques Toubon, former Minister of Culture, Moreau increased the number of loans for re-writing of scripts. The re-writing awards cannot be applied for, but may be granted by the Avances' commission instead of a production loan.

Moreau has been highly critical of both the state and status of screen writing in France. She also backed the Equinoxe writers' project (see Chapter 6 and Appendix C) and has done much to highlight the need for stronger development. In one speech that revealed her views on the subject, she asserted: 'If carpenters made chairs in the way that screenwriters produce scripts, we would all be sitting on the floor'.

The result of Moreau's tenure has been significant. Script re-writing awards increased from 10 in 1992 to 21 in 1993 and to a similar level in 1994/95. The overall monetary amounts for this area represented more than 40% of all projects funded through the 'Avances' scheme in 1993. In addition, 'Avances' is now using certain funds to send rejected screenplay writers on courses, including Sundance, Equinoxe and the Frank Daniel scriptwriting workshops. The writers are then encouraged to re-apply at a later date.

'Avances' is not the only state funder that is choosing to utilize these writing courses. British Screen, the Danish Film Institute and the Filmstiftung North Rhine-Westphalia (NRW) have either developed relationships with one of the above courses, or designed their own teaching sessions using professionals attached to the above. NRW also opened a permanent German film writing school in Cologne in December 1994.

France's other main development source for film is **PROCIREP**, one of France's authors' rights societies, which has a number of selective subsidy packages. Its feature film package allows CNC-registered companies which intend to produce a film of French nationality to apply for a scriptwriting bursary. Unlike nearly all support in France for film development, awards are for producers rather than just writers. It also takes a more liberal view on the language of a project, allowing companies to develop projects in languages outside French.

The work initiated by SCRIPT on supporting companies, rather than individual projects, has been taken on board by the CNC. **'Aide Au Développement' (AAD)** is probably the most important new strategy in the field of film development in France. The scheme, partly constructed and based on the results of SCRIPT's experience, was put into action by the CNC during 1994. But it also reflects a new view about development strategy in Europe.

Following a certain amount of Government pressure, the CNC decided to completely overhaul its AAD in 1993/94. The idea behind it is that the CNC should assist independent production companies with a 'treasury advance' at a time when they are taking maximum risk.

The new, fourth version of AAD has little in common with its previous incarnations. Since 1994, AAD money can only be spent on the script elements of a film's development. This includes: the purchase and optioning of rights, writing, rewriting, research of subject matter, translation and documentation. Pre-production costs – including location hunting, casting and legal expenses for finance – are not covered. The money is paid directly to producers, and not to directors/writers. Rather than necessarily being an enlightened, producer-led scheme, apparently the CNC feared a flood of unknown writers with no experience in film suddenly requesting finance. However, it is intended that these funds are subsequently passed on to writers, adaptors, dialogue developers and script editors, and are not to be used to cover a production company/producer's overhead.

Importantly, the AAD money is awarded as a repayable loan due in full on the first day of principal photography. This is a change from the previous system and clearly mirrors SCRIPT's system. However, unlike SCRIPT's Incentive Funding scheme, AAD also supports single projects – partly in an effort to stimulate young talent and new producers who tend to be excluded otherwise. The CNC sees the newly structured scheme as fitting between the developed project-stage finance offered by PROCIREP, and the support offered to projects through SCRIPT's Incentive Funding. Producers will also have to pay back part of the development loan if they go into production with a project within 18 months that was not presented for AAD development aid.

The newly structured AAD is clearly a critical junction for Europe's largest national public support system. Although the CNC is generally opposed to a widespread sprinkling of subsidy, it has indicated that over time, it expects the majority of the medium-sized independent production houses to be receiving AAD. The scheme's administrators said that they expect 50% of the projects backed not to make it into production. That is a very high success ratio, given that SCRIPT's scheme has been operating for more than 3 years, and is only now starting to reach a 25% development-into-production success ratio. However, the administrators hope that they will have made larger AAD allocations to the projects that are most likely to reach full production. By 1996, after 2 years of operation, an annual cash loss of 40% will be considered acceptable. Repayments of loans will remain within the AAD 'bank' and be added to income through the CNC's central funds.

3.3   THE UK

Although producers and writers clearly find development finance difficult to raise in the UK, there are considerable public and broadcasting sources available. However, the available funds are under considerable financial pressure, and competition to access development funds is very high. A further difficulty is that development funds which are cut off from production outlets tend to see less of their projects reach production. In contrast, broadcasters, the British Film Institute and British Screen develop material with writers and producers with a view to investing in the production. These sources of finance benefit from having both development and production funds available.

British Screen Finance is the most important national public support source for development. At the end of March 1991, the separate National Film Development Fund (NFDF) ceased to operate as a source of development finance. Its grant was passed to British Screen, which continues to support feature film development. British Screen's operation and strategy is different to the former NFDF's. According to British Screen's chief executive Simon Perry, the development loans are higher than those awarded by the former NFDF: 'We acknowledge that development is more expensive than the NFDF did, and we monitor our loans very closely'. Perry also pointed out that British Screen would greatly benefit from stronger links with and better access to script editors. British Screen's overall remit is to support both the development and production of projects which might otherwise not be made.

The reasons behind the above changes go some way to demonstrating the growing importance, both in terms of perception and practical support, of development. Simon Perry explains below the differences of strategy towards development between the old NFDF and British Screen.

> It seemed to me, when I went to British Screen in 1990, that it was a good moment to look at how the NFDF had been operating. We could then see in what ways it had been deficient and why, and what we should do to improve things in the future. [The change-over was made in March 1991.]

> There were two limitations on the success of the NDFD. One was that the amount of money available per project was unrealistically low. There were absolute ceilings on the amount that could be put into the development of any particular project. The normal maximum was around ECU 20 000, with the very distant possibility of a small supplementary loan beyond that in the case of 'highly deserving projects'. Those figures seemed to me to be absolutely out of touch with the real cost of development. Also, they bore no relation to the real cost of writers. While we obviously wanted to continue to encourage new writers, who might be able to be afforded with a loan of that kind, we wanted to encourage a range of writers, including experienced ones, to come and write the kinds of films that could be made in Europe, from Europe, and in which British Screen could eventually invest.

> The NFDF tended to pitch screenwriters and producers into a situation where they were developing in a vacuum. They would get the money, go off and write a first draft, and then couldn't get any further money from the NFDF. At that point they were orbiting in space. What I wanted to be able to do with potentially good projects was to say: We like it. Here is some money to write a first draft. If British Screen and the writer/producers all feel it's going well, then there is more money available for further development. The first loan is the first part of hopefully a range of phases.

> Without stating absolute ceilings, there is now more money than previously available under the NFDF. I also wanted to see that the projects in development with us were encouraged and developed by our staff; and that we consulted with them at every stage of development.

This way the producer/writer team knew they could come back for more money. They also knew that they were going to be quizzed, consulted and working in the development process with a partner that would take a view about putting money into the production. At the end of the day there's the possibility of British Screen finding up to 30% of the money for production. In the later stages of development we become part of financial planning of the project, with ideas about how to find and structure the finance of the film.

We have screenplay loans, which I hoped would become good enough for the project to become the recipient of a development loan. Then eventually it might get a preparation loan through to a production loan. The idea is to create a continuous passage for the projects that go well.

However, a balance needs to be struck here. We have to develop material without imposing on the producer, writer and director our own vision of the film. Neither can we insist that it has to be developed in our specific way or we wouldn't release any more development money. I think you can take those positions if you are a studio and are planning to finance the whole film, but I felt we shouldn't and couldn't do that. What we are looking for is a constant dialogue, a full exchange of ideas and mutual satisfaction as to the best way forward.

The **British Film Institute (BFI)**, the government supported film body, has a production arm. Its policy is to support experimental and new film work that would not otherwise be made by the marketplace. Through this grass-roots strategy, BFI Production has provided opportunities to first-time film-makers ranging from Ridley Scott to Derek Jarman alongside many other examples of young talent who have gone on to make films in the mainstream market. The production arm supports around a dozen low-budget feature length projects a year in active development. Each one receives a standard sum for two drafts and one polish. No money is given to producers, and in contrast to British Screen, which tends to either grant money to writers or producers, the money is writer/director-driven. It is highly competitive to access this development support. For example, each year between five and seven projects enter this development process, selected from the 500 submissions which are received every year.

The development/production success ratio normally results in one-in-two projects in development reaching production. According to Ben Gibson, the BFI's head of production, 'we never put a project into production which has not already had development support from us'. Typically, BFI-developed projects revert to other financiers in order to reach production. For example, they revert to the BBC or Channel 4, which repays the development costs without interest if they move into investing in a BFI project.

The **Scottish Film Production Fund/Glasgow Film Fund**, two of Scotland's key national and regional film support bodies, have together backed the development of around 30 films in 1993/94. Both funds are producer-driven, and both will support some overhead costs of producers. The Scottish Film Production Fund administers the Glasgow Film Fund.

3.4 GERMANY

Despite significant levels of scriptwriting finance and, to a lesser extent, development support, Germany has an uneven track record in development. Agents and distributors suggested that the problem has tended to lie with both the writers and the producers. Many screenwriters expect their scripts to be filmed in the form in which they are delivered to the producer; while producers have tended not to look for projects that could travel outside Germany. The result has been that a high percentage of films have found subsidy support but have gone into production before either they were fully developed or without any notion of what kind of audience they were aimed at.

Of the numerous support structures for German film-makers, there are two federal aid schemes for the film industry. These include (1) direct state aid funded from the treasury, under the jurisdiction of the Federal Ministry of the Interior, and (2) aid from the Federal Film Funding Institute (FFA). This has discretionary powers laid out in the 1986 Promotion and Development of Films Act to support the industry. It is funded from a levy on cinema turnover.

In addition, the individual 'laender', or states, offer a myriad of financial incentive schemes for film production within their areas. This aid includes loans, subsidies and grants. Overall, regional aid is directly linked with the promotion of employment and culture of that specific region. Put simply, if a fund invests in a film project, it will normally expect at least one-and-a-half times that sum to be spent in the region if the film enters in production.

However, significant changes have taken place recently, notably the setting up of the new Filmboard Berlin-Brandenburg in October 1994, and the newly constituted Filmförderungs GmbH (Hamburg Film Fund) in early 1995. A considerably more market-driven philosophy is being applied to project development under these funds. In addition, the Filmstiftung North Rhine-Westphalia is also looking to increase its level of support for development at all stages, including treatment, script and packaging.

The **Filmstiftung North Rhine-Westphalia (FNRW)** is a very significant new arrival since 1991 and has contributed heavily in terms of financial commitment to film, including investment in development of film projects. Producers and directors can apply, but they must be working with a screenwriter. Recipients of development funding have no legal claim to production support from the Fund, but it is generally understood that a project has a better chance of support as a 'known quantity', meaning that the Fund's selectors have already shown some commitment to its development, and hence have an incentive to support its production. This ties into the point made at the start of this chapter, namely that funds capable of investing beyond development are normally more committed and useful to producers compared to those that cannot.

The number of projects selected by NRW for script funding fell sharply between 1992 and 1994, because most of those submitted were of 'poor quality'. In April 1993, NRW's chief executive Dieter Kosslick declared at the MBS Master Class on Legal Aspects of Co-Production in Düsseldorf that the majority of screenplays sent to the Fund (more than 500 per year) were not up to standard. More time and more money should be invested by producers in the development of their feature projects.

Such public pronouncements are useful in two ways: they bring to the attention of producers what the perceived problems are with their development strategies; and they heighten the overall awareness of development as a key part of the film-making process.

Some of the key strategic thinking behind development has been carried out at NRW. Below, **Dieter Kosslick** explains recent changes to the NRW's development strategy.

At present, the fund spends money on scriptwriting and on development. This development money can apply to acquisition of rights and travel as well as scripts themselves.

The reason behind our present system is that the people who set up the fund were convinced that the industry has to spend much more money on development. We need to provide this money so that projects can come out of the ground. There was also an emphasis on looking to invest script money with a view to taking a production investment in projects. Once a script was written and developed, we could take a better look and see if we wanted to invest in it.

The Fund also wants to be able to assist producers as well as single writers in a larger way. We want to encourage development on a bigger scale. However, we only award secondary loans if we haven't spent our maximum amount, besides the applicant contributes their own investment on top. Phase loans – where smaller parts of money are released over a period of time – are rare, but they are possible.

For both script and larger development awards, we want to have a producer involved in the project. This is one of the biggest findings of the European Script Fund, which points to the importance of producers' driving projects forwards. I also think that SCRIPT demonstrates some of the problems of giving solitary writers loans which has proved how hard it is for a single writer to find producers and production finance, and get their scripts made. As a consequence, I am not so keen on the single script funding approach, because I think that if you give writers money, they need a framework.

After all the Fund's experience, including loans to writers, Frank Daniels workshops, and lots of seminars and other support, I supported the setting up of a special writing and development programme in Cologne, which started operating at the end of 1994. This will create a framework for people to work on a regular basis together with other professional teachers or writers for a certain period of time.

Experience shows that people need to be confronted by other professional writers and producers, and maybe distributors, to see the needs of all the different parts of the business encapsulated in one script. You need a controversial discussion about a script. The script may be good, but it needs an editor or other expert's input. However, this is a very un-European way of developing.

Scripts need to be targeted for a specific market. If you get the money and run, and then find an empty page in your typewriter, it can often lead to brilliant but unusable material. I think this framework would lead to a more realistic and supportive way of developing projects. We will build up a method where people are working on a day-to-day system. People will have access to editors and experienced professionals. Sales companies and distributors should come into the process at a later stage.

What we are thinking of moving towards in the future is to offer only development money. Then the applicants can decide on where it needs to go. Single script money will not be available. To access the development money, you have to be either from FNRW or linked to someone with the area, i.e. offer a project co-financed or co-produced with a partner. Otherwise everyone will show up and take our development money and run off with it without benefitting the region. Part of the problem for funding systems is the temptation to stay with the same people, but if we are really serious about discovering talent in this area, then we must take risks.

We don't have an incentive funding system like SCRIPT. But we have introduced a different kind of incentive system. If you make a successful movie with our development and production money, then although the FNRW share is recouped, we won't actually take it. Instead, we will give it back to the producer on a revolving account. They can then decide what to develop with this money. Once the new scripts are developed, we will then have a look at it for potential investment.

One of the most interesting new developments in Germany has been the launch of the **Filmboard Berlin-Brandenburg**. Although script development and pre-production support was available from both the two former regional sources up to the end of 1993, the funds were brought together as the Filmboard Berlin-Brandenburg GmbH in 1994. The new Fund, which has been operating since September 1994, now has ECU 2–2.5m funds for development, along with other support mechanisms. Under the new Fund's executive director, Klaus Keil, at least 10% of its annual ECU 24m budget has been set aside for development and pre-production. Keil has made a considerable impact on producers by taking a more 'market-led' approach to the fund's operations.

The new approach has clearly been influenced by SCRIPT's experience, alongside the problems encountered by fellow German subsidy support mechanisms. **Klaus Keil** outlines below his views on development:

Development is very, very high on our list of priorities at the Filmboard. The story is the basis for everything: all the energy, imagination, lifeblood and money in a feature film production.

The absurd thing is that the importance of development has never been acknowledged here in Germany. The concept of professionally working on scripts is only very slowly being adopted in our film and television industry. In Germany, the notion is still held that a screenplay is a piece of literature, and hence a work of art which can only be altered by the creator. This is really a scandalous attitude. It may be an appropriate attitude in certain individual cases, but it does not apply to the majority of film projects.

All the millions piled up in film funds are therefore a waste of time if the script isn't up to scratch. The importance of script and project development has to be driven into people's heads before other areas can change, and hence why I will make sure development plays a key role at the Filmboard. I will be encouraging established producers, but also particularly the young, offbeat and crazy to submit their ideas and win development support from Berlin-Brandenburg.

I believe that if you spend around ECU 50 000 on the development of a project, you can see whether the market has a place for it or not. If I spend a million marks on development, then I can develop 10 projects, and risk it coming to nothing. But if I put one million into just one project, then the money has been risked on just one film, not ten. I think that approaching development here with a view to spreading the risk over a 1:10 ratio will prove worthwhile.

A new Hamburg film funding body called **Filmförderungs GmbH** was established by late 1995. The new state-run body took over from the existing Hamburg Film Office and the Hamburg Film Fund, and has an annual funding budget of nearly ECU 8.3m. The new fund will be dedicating around 15% of its budget to development, 70% to production and 15% to distribution. Selection decisions will be made by a three-strong committee. Around 15% of the overall budget will be allocated to low-budget and experimental projects. (See Practical Guide.)

3.5 SPAIN

In contrast to France, the UK and Germany, there are considerably less public development funds in Spain. In essence, the development financier is the screenplay writer who either defers payment or is simply not paid for his or her work. This deferment of payment still allows the producer to work with a script to raise finance and generate development on a project. However, the whole concept of development beyond just a script is highly 'underdeveloped' in the EU's southern states, and Spain is no exception.

The **Spanish Film Institute (ICAA)** – under the wing of the Spanish Ministry of Culture – does not grant development money for producers. However, it does operate a 'film protection fund' which has operated through the advancement of funds to producers, with a maximum per film of 50% of its budget, up to a limit of ECU 1.2m.

The ICAA supported the production of 33 films a year from 1991 to 1993. Because the Ministry is slow in administering the money, a contractual agreement was set up with the Banco Exterior de España (BEX). This oversees low-interest loans to producers, based on the government subsidy allowance, to be repaid by means of a graduated scale amount from box-office returns. However, the majority of these loans are never repaid, as box-office revenue margins are virtually never met. Spanish producers are heavily dependent on subsidy funds, with 72% of films produced in 1993 receiving Ministerial support.

A new policy was introduced in 1994 to grant incentive money to packages of three films from a producer; a model that has certain similarities to the SCRIPT's Incentive Funding scheme (see Chapter 6). However, although the Ministry's new policy is clearly aimed at moving away from project-by-project funding, the funds are not strictly 'development' finance. The subsidy still operates as an advance for pre-production.

New regulations from the Ministry of Culture regarding subsidies for 1995 have included a change in the administration of these advances to producers. Advance subsidies for feature films are now limited to relatively new directors who have made no more than two films previously. A total of ECU 4.6m in advance money has been set for 1995 and the funds will only be applied to low-budget features. However, exceptional projects may benefit from support granted on an exceptional basis. The purpose behind the new policy is to promote new and younger film-makers, and to limit the dependency of experienced Spanish producers on state funds. By effectively encouraging these producers to look to private finance and money from abroad, the Ministry is hoping to stimulate the private-sector market.

The ICAA does also operate a special subsidy fund for writers. Established in 1990, it is worth ECU 350 000 annually and has been renewed in 1995 and 1996. The money is strictly grants for writers and not subsidy funding for fully-fledged development. It does not have to be repaid. Producers have been pushing to get this grant considered as payment for a script, in an effort to save monies. Writers are understandably against this. As Spanish screenwriter and Iberoamericana executive Antonio Saura points out: 'Although producers are pushing to have this money considered as payment for a script, so that they would not have to pay any further fee to the writer, writers are vehemently refusing this'.

Overall, it is another strong example of seed money to writers not actually resulting in projects completed. Almost none of the 90 awarded screenplays have been made into films. This 'single writing' problem also comes up in other national funds, and most notably in the experience of the European Script Fund. The problem of awarding money to writers in a vacuum should not be underestimated. The Spanish experience again underlines the alienation of writers to the production process, a problem that continually results in scripts aimed at no particular audience or market.

A recent change in policy in regional film support took place in Catalunya, with significant new monies being released for film development. In February 1995, Joan Guitart, the Catalan Minister of Culture of the Generalitat de Catalunya, announced new guidelines for support to Catalan film and TV makers. For the first time, they included a specific allocation, ECU 205 000, for development funding, of which applicants may apply for up to ECU 17 000 per project.

According to official data for 1993 and 1994 from the Spanish Ministry of Culture, which provides a general indication of trends rather than specific numbers, directors continue to dominate the Spanish feature film development process. The study compares the UK, France and Spain. See Tables 2 and 3 and Figures 4 and 5. In summary, the data shows that:

- Spanish directors are involved with writing the script far more than in France or the UK.
- The director is involved in co-writing the script more than in the UK but about the same as in France.
- Relatively few Spanish films are written by an outside writer, compared with the UK and France.
- Few Spanish films are made where the producer is involved with the script.

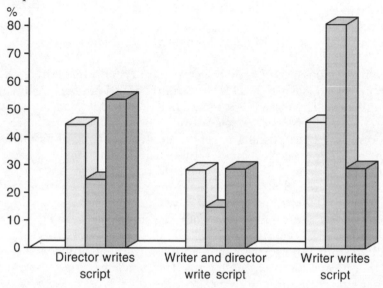

Figure 3 Comparison of French (□), British (▨) and Spanish (▨) projects in development 1994

Table 2 Comparison of France, Spain and UK projects in development 1994

	France (%)	UK (%)	Spain (%)
Projects where director writes script	39	17.5	50
Projects where writer and director co-write script	23	8.5	22.7
Projects where just writer writes script	38	74	27.27
Projects with director, writer and producer attached	42	48	27.27

Source: European Film File/Screen International I.C.A.A.

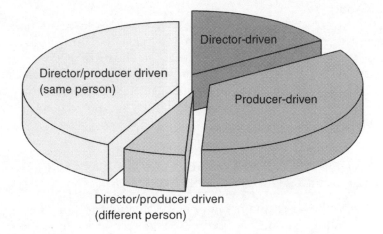

Director-driven

Director/producer driven
(same person)

Producer-driven

Director/producer driven
(different person)

Figure 4 Percentage breakdown of Spanish film production 1994
Source: MBS research/ICAA/Spanish Ministry of Culture

Table 3 Percentage breakdown of Spanish film productions 1994

Director-driven	21%
Director/producer-driven (same person)	36%
Director/producer-driven (different person)	12%
Producer-driven	31%

3.6   ITALY

Although Spain may appear weak in terms of development support, Italy is the most glaring example of all the Latin states of an industry with no policy towards development whatsoever.

There are no development finance mechanisms available from public support systems in Italy. A very small amount of money is awarded each year to just five scriptwriters through a private foundation scheme, **Premio Solinas** (see Appendix A for details). Although very prestigious, this source is understandably limited.

The lack of state support for film development was not addressed in the new film law. On February 23, 1994, the Italian Parliament passed a new film law, the first in 25 years. Although set to alter radically the way state subsidies are distributed, no provision for development financing was included.

There is a high level of criticism concerning this omission. The new law provides for the support of 15–20 films per year. Italian producer Enzo Porcelli, of Aliza Film, suggested the state would be better off financing 10 films and developing 50 projects. However, producers and film-making bodies in Italy tend to concentrate on production finance to the exclusion of development.

The only provision in the new law that relates to development is a screenplay prize. Ironically, the law requires that the competing scripts are complete when submitted for consideration. The prize will be awarded to 'screenplay writers who contribute to the growth of the Italian cinema's artistic and cultural heritage'. The number of prize winners and the amount of the prizes are decided every 2 years by decree and winners are chosen by committee.

3.7   NATIONAL SOURCES OF DEVELOPMENT FINANCE IN SMALLER TERRITORIES ACROSS EUROPE

Both the Netherlands and Ireland have recently been stimulated by new public funding institutions. The following section looks at the reasons behind these new approaches, and then examines public funding support in certain other smaller territories.

3.7.1   THE NETHERLANDS

From November 1, 1993, the new **Nederlands Fonds voor de Film** (Dutch Film Fund) effectively swallowed two existing funds, the former Dutch Film Fund and the Film Production Fund. The new Fund was set up on the initiative of the Dutch Minister of Culture. Additional public money was invested in the operation, giving a total of about ECU 7.85m, nearly ECU 1.6m more than the two previous funds combined.

However, according to the Dutch Film Fund's chief executive Ryclef Rienstra, central costs effectively take up most of the advantages that might have been gained financially from the merger because the new fund has more responsibilities than the previous two together. As part of its preparation to form new film legislation, the government commissioned a major report, *Stimulating Audiovisual Production in the Netherlands* (McKinsey & Co., January 1993), examining and contrasting in detail the European and Dutch audiovisual industries.

While the McKinsey report raised numerous points, it emphasized the crucial role of development in the successful building of any film industry's infrastructure. Potential strengthening actions included:

- 'Selectively awarding larger amounts for scripts supported by established producers'.
- 'Providing "seed capital" directly to new scriptwriters'.

The alleged benefits of introducing the above elements were:

- 'Improving audience and expert appreciation of films' (in other words, finding a market for films by improving their quality).
- 'Increasing script applications and hence selectivity'.
- 'Providing increased opportunity for new writers'.

Specifically, at the script/development stage, the report recommended that the maximum amount of subsidy per script could be selectively increased by 200% to 300% from the pre-1994 levels (see Directory, Appendix A for further application details).

Ryclef Rienstra was closely involved in the establishing the policy of the new Dutch Film Fund (DFF). Below he explains how the new DFF approached development funding during its inception:

The major difference between the new DFF and the previous two separate funds is that producers and film-makers all complained that there was too little money for the development and production of films. A major motive behind the merger is that we now can look at a whole range of projects – ranging from small, experimental and art, through to higher-budget theatrical films – at the same time.

One of the major policy elements that emerged from the research and debate over setting up the new fund was that too many producers were forced to produce their films to survive. The previous Funds had been too soft, and supported productions that were not really ready.

We decided to put more emphasis on the development of films, and to try to make more selection in the development phase. This way, we could try to narrow awards down to a smaller number actually backed in production, and give a higher amount per film. We have decided on taking a broad policy towards feature film development. We want a stronger emphasis on the role of the producer, hence no application is possible without the involvement of a professional producer.

This early involvement of the producer means that the development of the script will be more thorough, and the selection will have already have taken place in the development phase. Why? Because if the producer wants to go into production, the money from our fund is not enough. They will have to find other money to produce the film.

The Fund will also encourage producers in development to cancel the film if it proves to be a weak project. The Fund has three main people overseeing the system, but if in our view there is no market for the project, we will stop the development support.

The new push towards development is reflected partly in the higher levels we can allocate. The previous maximum amount allocated to a writer was rather low; and the involvement of the producer was hardly recognized.

Initial requests will now be looked at by a committee, which will decide if it is viable for development support. A number of stages will follow, starting with an allocation of money for the first draft. Further 'second stage' support for more drafts may be applied for; and a script analysis can be requested. If we have faith in the project, support for the producer in the form of a sum covering some of the costs of the project package can be applied for. Producers will have to raise at least 20% of the development costs themselves.

In addition to single project support, we have taken SCRIPT's Incentive Funding scheme, and applied it slightly differently. It is aimed at more established producers. We will award ECU 120 000 for three projects over 2 years, rather than three projects a year as in SCRIPT's scheme. The major problem for producers is that so few of them have any real assets in terms of rights. This leaves them in a weak negotiating position and is something we are actively trying to change. We are also trying to select fewer producers, and build up individual ones. If a producer has a track record, it is easier to find finance.

The problem with development is not the quantity of the projects, which are plentiful, but their quality. In Holland we have a lot of projects in development, but not enough consideration about their real potential. Development requires a careful business plan, where a producer considers: Where do I start? Where do I raise my seed money from? What can I offer financiers? From the DFF's point of view, we ask: 'What will be the result of our development investment?'.

3.7.2   IRELAND

In contrast to the Netherlands, which has had a relatively consistent policy toward feature film support, Ireland's recent history is one of much policy debate and recent change. Nevertheless, it is a strong example of a territory which has recently re-introduced public support for the film industry with beneficial effect. In contrast to the former public support strategy, development is now playing a key role in its operations.

The **Irish Film Board (IFB)** was disbanded in 1987. According to sources who worked closely with the Board, of its annual budget of ECU 630 000, about 10% was spent on development support. Individual loans were nevertheless quite high, with top loans for development reaching ECU 63 000–94 000 in some cases. The Department of Arts, Culture and the

Gaeltacht reconstituted the IFB in April 1993. From 1987 to 1993, no substantial development support from the state was forthcoming. Part of the new significance development has played was due to the role played by SCRIPT during the period 1989–1993, when no other development finance was available for Irish producers. SCRIPT's activity raised the profile of development during this period.

Although there is no separate budget or allocated quota set for development, the Board spent around ECU 280 000 of its annual 1993 budget of ECU 1.15m on development. By 1994 the annual budget rose to ECU 2.4m, of which around ECU 360 000 was directed towards development. A similar 15% figure was spent throughout 1995, although the Board stresses that this figure is flexible rather than a fixed percentage.

'Given that the IFB was reconstituted after a lapse of 5 years, the board specifically adopted the strategy of developing widely and broadly', explained IFB chief executive Rod Stoneman. 'In our first year we tended to support development with small amounts of seed money. Now we are becoming more stringent'.

The reasons behind increasing the IFB's commitment to development were:

- To stimulate proper preparation of projects that the Board might consider supporting in production (10% of a total budget).
- To help boost Irish producers' opportunities of raising film finance from other sources, notably from Europe.
- To stimulate and train the development of Irish film talent.
- To provide an initial provision for the continuity of production and availability of Irish films.
- To encourage the making of Irish stories both at home and to international audiences.

Although the Irish Film Board is clearly the largest and most important source of development finance in Ireland, **Filmbase** (backed by RTE) also offers some support on a much smaller scale. Filmbase, a cultural initiative that supports Ireland's writers and directors, offered a substantial increase in the level of awards to scripts for short films in 1993, backing six projects with awards of up to ECU 40 000.

3.7.3 OTHER SMALLER TERRITORIES

While most of the EU's smaller territories obviously invest a lower volume of public finance in film development, on a proportional basis the levels are significantly higher than certain of Europe's larger territories. Scandinavian countries, for example, have a far more organized and structured approach towards development than Spain or Italy. Others have taken on board the example shown by SCRIPT, the NRW and British Screen, and have started to invest in script workshops and the training of producers in development techniques. Greece, a territory with a long history of 'auteur-driven' development approach, is a case in point (again, practical information can be found in the Directory of Contacts at the back of this book.)

Belgium's film support systems are divided into two key areas: Ministry for Cultural Affairs and Ministry for Flemish Cultural Affairs. These reflect the linguistic division in the country, although the funding mechanisms are similar (but not identical) for both the Flemish-speaking Flanders in the North and the French-speaking Wallonia in the South. Both Funds are geared exclusively toward supporting domestic producers who are making films in their respective language. This is a fairly typical strategy that fits most of the smaller countries' public development models.

According to the Flemish Ministry, scriptwriters have been able to apply for grants of up to ECU 7500 per project from a total development budget of around ECU 102 000. The ministry estimates that owing to recent changes, this overall figure will be 'slightly bigger', but spending will depend on the number of scripts supported. In 1993, 10 screenplays were given support. According to producer Erwin Provoost, all scripts presented for development support are ultimately searching for production finance from the same source, namely the Ministry's funds.

Belgium's French-speaking funding is significantly larger than its Flemish counterpart. From a total budget of ECU 3.5m, about ECU 500 000 is available for development funding, but this includes features, shorts and documentaries. The concept of 'matching fund', where the producer has to share 50% of the development costs, is applied. This follows the EU's policy guidelines where, for example, all MEDIA Programme support has to be matched by 50% funding for all its activities and investments.

According to administrator Henri Roanne, the French-speaking rules changed in 1994. Previously the terms were very favourable to the producer, who had to reimburse just 10% of the grant to the fund. Now the 50% development loan has to be repaid on the first day of principal photography. Grants are also available from both funds for 'cultural films' which are highly specific in language and subject matter to their region. Both the French-speaking and the Flemish funding bodies each give an annual prize for the best script.

In **Greece**, the key source of development finance is the Greek Film Centre (GFC), which has been established since 1986 as a private company, but all stock is owned by the Greek government. It is essentially the main co-producer of all Greek film productions.

According to Eugenia Liroudia, who heads up the development section of the GFC, 'it is important to understand that the scriptwriter does not exist in Greece. We have a huge literary tradition, but no screenwriting tradition. The European Script Fund has definitely helped us in terms of the idea of crossing borders. The development department here is trying to do the same – create situations and stories, and talk to people who are more experienced'.

In an effort to put a new policy towards development into practice, the GFC, in collaboration with the Greek Ministry of Culture and the House of Fine Arts and Letters, held its first 'Greek Script Workshop', titled the 'Script House', in November/December 1994. The objective was to 'contribute to the improvement of scriptwriting as well as the further development of the film project from the idea stage to pre-production'. The 'Script House' operated through a combination of workshops, lectures, screenings and script analyses. Domestic and international experts in the fields of scriptwriting and script analysis attended.

Virtually the only source of development funding for feature films in **Portugal** is the State. The country normally produces up to 10 films a year, but 1993 was a setback, with just four films completed. The Portuguese Film Institute – Instituto Portugues De Arts Cinematograficas (IPACA) – supports the development of up to six scripts a year, with ECU 6000–7000 being loaned to the screenwriter. Subsidies are also available to producers for the development of six to eight features.

Unlike the majority of public support systems, payments by the IPACA are not considered a development loan. Instead they are both non-repayable grants. The situation is largely unchanged in terms of the level of development support available from the State, which has at least kept in line with inflation. The IPACA is currently reconsidering its grant situation and may introduce a repayable loan system. According to IPACA's vice-president Salvato Telles De Meneses, it is likely that a larger number of films can be supported in this way. The Institute is not happy with the current system because it 'creates too much dependency' on public sources of finance.

The five main **Scandinavian** countries are relatively small when viewed as separate film markets. As a consequence, co-productions and public-sector support play an important financial underpinning role in every territory. Economically, it is effectively impossible to move a film into production in any one territory without relying on state support. Each country has a national film fund, and the region overall has a pan-Scandinavian fund, the Nordic Film and TV Fund. While pan-Scandinavian production funding has been a typical feature of film finance, co-development between the territories is a more recent trend, especially in the case of larger projects intended for the pan-Scandinavian market.

The Nordic Film and TV Fund was set up in 1990 with the aim to support Nordic co-productions. Between 1990 and 1993, nearly 150 films were given support, including 57 features. However, according to the Fund's former executive, Bengt Forslund, the Board decided in 1993 to stop providing development finance (for around 10–15 projects a year). 'As all Nordic Film Institutes now have development money – and producers can apply to the

European Script Fund – we decided to stop spending money on development', he explained. The key point is that development finance is available at a national level, with the Nordic Fund operating mostly as a 'top-up' financier rather than a provider of 'seed money'.

The Swedish Film Institute is the key public source of funding in **Sweden**. Following the 1992 Film, Television and Video agreement signed by the government and representatives of the Swedish audiovisual industry, 75% of all public funds go to 'advance support' (development and production) and 25% for 'retroactive support' (distribution).

The advance support scheme generated around ECU 7.8m in 1994, of which 10% was invested in development – mostly in scripts. Hence the figure for public support for development is around ECU 780 000, a very significant figure. The old system had approximately the same budget levels for development.

There are two consultants for features, who analyse all applications and oversee the Institute's funding for films. Each one allocates around 30–40 smaller development awards, 15–20 slightly larger awards and pre-production support to five to six feature films a year. Independent companies approach the Institute for support and can receive the larger levels. Occasionally a major company, a TV channel and a consultant from the Institute will co-develop a project together, although the independent company will run the production.

The overall emphasis has not changed since Sweden joined the MEDIA Programme in May 1994 and gained access to SCRIPT. According to the Swedish MEDIA Desk, there has been 'a strong and steady demand for information on SCRIPT within the local film industry'.

The **Danish Film Institute** (DFI) is a key example of a public body undergoing a major change in policy towards development. At the end of 1993 the Institute decided to quadruple the amount of money allocated to development. From a total annual budget of around ECU 9.24m, it invested just ECU 132 000–200 000 in development of projects. This rose to ECU 660 000 in 1994.

Previous figures show that in 1991, 1.5% of the DFI's total budget was spent on the development of 32 projects, and a further 5.5% on pre-production support. In 1992, the percentage for development decreased to 1.4% of the overall budget, with 41 films supported. The percentage climbed in 1993, with 2.3% of the total budget being spent on development. Pre-production loans are theoretically repayable if the film goes into profit.

Former DFI director Henrik Bering-Liisberg said he hoped that the higher level of development money would mean stronger scripts, and would also encourage companies to spend more time and thought on the packaging and pre-production stage, rather than pressing to get into production. The Institute has become more circumspect about the quality of projects it decides to support through to the production stage.

In addition to the Institute, a new Danish Television Fund has been established. It became a matter of some controversy how this new ECU 6m Fund (over 2 years) raised through the TV license fee would operate. Hopes that it would top up the amount of public money for development to a total figure of ECU 1.8m were unfounded, as the money went to production.

Public funds in **Norway** have provided a steady annual sum of around ECU 358 000 since 1990/91 onwards. These are broken down into three main sources.

Norsk Film is a leading Norwegian company that is 66% government owned and 33% owned by a cinema exhibition chain. Norsk Film produces around three films a year. Although fixed amounts are set aside for script development including features and further project development, the company received permission to switch more money into development from 1993 onwards. According to Norsk producer Harald Ohrvik, the company works on around 50 projects over a 2-year period, but it only moves six to seven into 'full development'.

The Norwegian Film Institute (NFI) tends to demand a finished script before supporting projects, although it does have a budget for pre-production support. Money for script development is not repayable, but if a film goes into production its original investment will be deducted from any further funding. According to NFI executive, Jan Erik Holst, around 10 scripts are submitted for each one that is produced. He argues the ratio should be higher, 50:1. 'We give too little to too many, and are considering taking more money from production and putting it into development. We would like to have two levels of support, and perhaps make an annual payment for 2 to 3 years to good writers'.

Other funds include the National Centre for Screen Studies, which has a fund for script development; and the Norwegian Cassette Fund (raised by a tax on blank tapes). This is mostly spent on short films, but it can award significant sums for development (see Appendix A).

The Finnish Film Foundation is the single most important source of film finance in **Finland**, handling production and development subsidies in the form of soft loans, repayable if a film goes into profit. This is most unlikely to happen. For example, the 1992 Finnish comedy *Numbskull Emptybrook, President of the Republic of Finland* was the most successful domestic film in 1992, but failed to recoup its costs.

The annual budget of the Foundation has dropped considerably since 1991's total budget of ECU 11m to approximately ECU 8m in 1994 for development and production. The Foundation supported 14 feature films in 1993, spending a total of ECU 6m, of which about 20% was spent on development and pre-production. According to successful producer applicants, grants per screenplay used to be worth around ECU 12 000, but have now dropped to around ECU 7000.

Other sources include AVEK, a promotion centre for Audiovisual

Culture in Finland, funded by a Finnish tax on videotapes. Although this centre had ECU 2m in 1993, most of it was spent on short films and documentaries.

The public support for films in **Iceland** is divided into two sectors. The Icelandic Film Fund, started in 1979, is funded mainly through a cinema ticket levy (1984 film law). The aid is given in the form of subsidies or loans for filming. The majority of the aid is direct subsidy and is administered project by project. Over the last 5 years, 21 applicants to the Fund have been given support for the development of their feature film projects.

Other sources include the Cultural Fund of Radio Stations which gives grants in the audiovisual sector. The bulk of this money is development aid, although there is no breakdown between production and development.

3.7.4   CENTRAL AND EASTERN EUROPE

The transition of the film industry in Central and Eastern Europe from state monopoly to private enterprise that began in 1989 has signalled an end to state support for film production. Insufficient government subsidies and a lack of entrepreneurial, privately financed producers to fill the gap have resulted in a decline in production across the entire region.

Feature film development in the Western European sense did not exist under the old system. The new Central and Eastern European producer has to learn a new vocabulary of terms, including 'options', 'rights', 'development budget', 'pre-sales' and other development and pre-production requisites. These activities are currently being executed under very low or 'no-budget' financial circumstances.

Under the state studio system, screenwriters and directors were full-time employees who turned out treatments, scripts and developed projects for production on a regular basis, regardless of the potential market or audience. The director-driven 'auteur' system has been the traditional creative lynchpin, with most directors writing their own material. Some have teamed up with professional screenplay writers, including the late Krzysztof Kieslowski and Krzysztof Piesiewicz, but most product has been artistically driven.

With few exceptions, directors worked with other studio employees developing their projects. Salaried screenplay writers were employed by the studios to turn out treatments and scripts, regardless of whether or not the films were approved for production. Once a project received the green light, production went ahead with little regard for schedules.

Screenplays would often be little more than a rough outline. The director would improvise depending on creative whims as the filming progressed, which could take up to a year. Rights, options and future distribution were all handled by the state. The cost of such relative creative freedom was that the authorities would exercise stringent censorship over the content of the film. Directors could be banned from working under the state studio system if they stepped out of line. However, authorities relaxed somewhat during the years leading up to 1989, offering film-makers heavy support and little interference.

Successful film development has faced major difficulties during the troubled transition period after 1989. The state studios that turned out large numbers of features, shorts, documentaries and animation, have subsequently been cut adrift from subsidy funding. They continue as private enterprises, or as underfunded, struggling facilities houses. All creative personnel, including directors, scriptwriters, designers and cameramen are no longer salaried and depend on freelance work. Very low levels of state subsidies are now awarded on a project-by-project basis. These are mostly granted to independent production companies which utilize the former state facilities.

The majority of the funding bodies in Central and Eastern European states (see Appendix B for details) award grants on the basis of treatments, screenplays or partially developed projects submitted to an elected industry board. Usually, those with potential receive a small grant for further development or for a part of the overall production budget that is to be augmented by a private producer or a foreign entity such as the CNC or one of the MEDIA projects.

Programmes such as the East West Producers' Seminars, currently on hold, run by UK producer Lynda Myles and Katya Krausova, have helped transfer some of the skills needed by the new breed of eastern producer. Although projects were not specifically developed throughout the seminars themselves, producers and executives benefited through the contact with Western producers, lawyers, agents and film bodies. For example, Vaclav Marhoul, the reinstated head of Barrandov Film Studios, attended the seminars in 1991.

In addition, a number of programmes to encourage more professional training and execution of screenplay writing, such as the Hartley-Merril Awards and Workshops, have been implemented. However, attempts to train screenwriters to concentrate on more potentially commercial ideas, along with efforts to guide auteur-driven directors towards the audience have largely proved futile.

However, the development process is still tending to originate largely with the director. Working with a producer who has creative input as well as providing money is still a new concept, and has encountered considerable resistance in many of the central and eastern territories.

Part of the overriding feeling from the majority of local film-makers is that it would be a mistake to destroy the auteur system and replace it with a more commercial production approach. This may explain why the French, with their emphasis on the auteur system, have had the greatest success in cooperating with these territories. Co-production has proved to be one way of solving the production finance problems and many foreign funds and producers are increasingly willing to become involved at the development stage of projects.

However, research indicates that the general consensus is that the film industry in these territories will continue to depend on subsidized funding to survive, and that development money will need to come from government sources. Critically, generalizations about the Central and Eastern European states are unhelpful. The following breakdown and interviews with professionals point to a considerable variety of situations in the different states.

The **Central and Eastern Europe** states are profiled below.

The public agency Roskomkino is the main source of public development funding in the **CIS** and the **Baltic States**. Overall, Roskomkino has participated in around 50% of the films made last year, partially funding more than 70 titles. Projects are submitted to the agency by individuals normally on the basis of a treatment or a full script, with a board deciding which project to fund.

Overall, a lack of strong screenplay writing and professionally trained producers is seen as one of the most pressing needs. Directors remain reluctant to share control of a project. However, younger directors such as Valery Todorovsky (*Love and Katerina Ismailova*) are setting up their own production companies, and developing their own projects alongside new young producers with a combination of private and public funding. Development financing outside Russia itself and the Baltics is at present virtually non-existent and mostly in the hands of the former state studios or private entrepreneurs, neither whom have much money for production, let alone development finance.

The only source of public development funding in **Hungary** is the Hungarian Motion Picture Foundation, which has come in for heavy criticism recently. Founded in 1991 to channel professional and financial support for Hungarian film-makers, the foundation is responsible for all aspects of funding. Most development is nurtured in the studios, which are now made up of independent production companies who are still dependent on state support for survival. The Foundation's board chooses which projects to fund on the basis of the scripts submitted. Money for private development is virtually impossible to attract.

More than half the budgets of **Poland**'s 29 features produced in 1993 were supported by government subsidy. Television also played a key role, acting as a co-producer on a high level of projects and financing around 40% of the features produced that year. The system of subsidies is divided between three key grant agencies: one deals with script, one with production and one with distribution. Founded in 1991, the script agency has received more than 300 script applications for all films, of which half have received support.

The production agency evaluates applications received from producers that have already undergone the initial stages of development. The producer must be able to raise at least 30% of the project's budget. While most of the Polish film community has reacted favourably to the work of the government agencies, the script agency has been considered the weakest link. Once again, this is mainly due to the screenplay writer being traditionally viewed as the poor cousin of the director in Poland.

The **Czech Republic** has benefited from a much stronger tradition of screenwriting than in most other central and eastern European countries. As a consequence, an emphasis has been placed on the early development stages. Development funding comes from both private and public sources (see Directory of Contacts for details). There were 22 features produced in the Czech Republic in 1993, with five reaching the Czech box-office top 10. While rising costs make it hard for production companies to see a return of their money, they are still investing their own capital and attracting a range of other investment.

Despite severe financial difficulties, 15 features were produced in 1993 in **Romania**. In the absence of private funding and poor box-office commercial prospects, responsibility for development and production funding of feature films remains largely in the hands of the National Centre for Cinematography. This body selects projects on the basis of artistic merit and export potential. Little direct development finance is available.

In **Bulgaria**, film production has slumped from 40 features annually in 1990 to just six in 1993. The number of cinemas has dropped from 3140 to 105, with attendances dropping from 45 to 7 million over just 4 years. With inflation at 2000% in the same period, it is not surprising that there is little money for development. The director's 'auteur' ascendancy is paramount in Bulgaria, with little work written by screenwriters alone. Literary improvisations are commonplace.

Hungarian film-maker **Istvan Szabo** explains below the situation in Hungary with regards to screenwriting and approaches to feature film development.

The situation in Hungary is not very good. Previously, the Hungarian film industry was 100% subsidized by the Ministry of Culture. But the system has changed and we now have the Hungarian Film Foundation which is responsible for administering film subsidies. The biggest problem is that it is the only source of money for developing screenplay material, and is clearly not enough. The Foundation is not willing to support young film-makers or projects in the first stages of development. It does not tend to support projects that have some new values or that are not so visibly interesting.

There are no private sources for development. There are no people in Hungary that are ready to throw money out of the

window. Films find it almost impossible to be commercially successful because the domestic market is too small. A Hungarian film
can be successful commercially only if the film can reach other
countries too, but that is very limited owing to the language being
very difficult.

To reach other pan-European support mechanisms, you still have
to go through the Foundation. I think this is very bad, because they
act as the official body for the country's national film industry, but
are working in exactly the same way as the former office of the
Ministry of Culture under the old regime.

Some directors write their own scripts, and others work with a
scriptwriter, but the problem is that we don't have really good
screenplay writers. Perhaps we need a special fund to encourage
screenwriters and for promoting script development.

Polish film-maker **Krzysztof Zanussi** explains below the situation in
Poland with regards to screenwriting and approaches to feature film
development.

Polish film has found its way under the new conditions. Public film
agencies were founded to support film with public money and
these agencies have worked very well. I cannot complain about the
amount of money that is given to film development, which is
appropriate both for production and development, given the economic problems that our country is experiencing.

The levels have declined since the communist times (when 40–50
films a year were produced), but we are still shooting around 20
films a year in Poland. This change is not as dramatic as it sounds, and
other neighbouring countries are envious of our production opportunities. However, we still have to look for collaboration abroad for
more than half of our productions, and foreign co-producing partners are often involved from the beginning of the development
phase.

Polish subsidy is divided among three key government agencies:
a script agency; a production agency and a distribution agency.
Both the script and the production agencies play a role in the
development stages of a project. The script agency refunds the
producer the project's development costs if the treatment submitted is accepted by the board of directors of the script fund. It is
modelled on a slightly similar basis to the European Script Fund,
where the producer is expected to provide additional money for
development if he/she receives money from the fund.

However, the people who have been sitting on public boards
which are deciding who gets the public funding should now be
scrutinized simply because they have been in place for 2 years.

Most Polish directors write their own scripts just as in France, Germany or in Italy. That's a very continental approach, and everything you see subsidized is in the auteur line of work. But it's not always good. We now have some emerging scriptwriters who simply don't want to direct films. But they are in the minority. I think the number of scriptwriters needs to rise.

KEY SUMMARY POINTS

1. There has been a rise of nearly ECU 12m in the EU's public-sector spending on film development. Given that the combined public sources of the UK, Germany and France amounted to around ECU 6m in 1994, the level of new money made available specifically for development is considerable.
2. Public development funds across Western Europe are nationally specific and, hence, tend to support screenwriters and producers who are mostly working in their domestic language. However, larger German funds have started to back the development of projects in the English language (notably NRW and Filmboard Berlin-Brandenburg). With the exception of PROCIREP, French development support remains almost exclusively dedicated towards French-language projects.
3. Europe's Latin territories remain at a considerable disadvantage due to their present attitude towards development. Despite certain gradual changes in Spain and Greece, Italy remains the worst example of a high-producing nation with no policy towards development.
4. There has been a considerable rise in the public support for script and development training and workshops. This trend has ranged from the UK, Germany, France through to Scandinavia and Greece. It complements work done on a pan-European level by the Media Business School, the training and research arm of the MEDIA Programme, through its different initiatives (see Chapter 6).
5. Eastern and Central Europe is only now starting to consider how to support its national film industries after the revolution. However, development support and training for screenwriters remains limited. The traditional 'auteur' approach to writing and directing remains dominant.

Broadcasters' support systems

4

Television broadcasters across Europe do play a role in the financing of feature film development. However, their involvement varies greatly from institution to institution, and from territory to territory. Some, like the UK's Channel 4 and France's Canal Plus, spend tranches of their film production/investment budgets directly on independent film development. However, many broadcaster executives expect the independent producer to bring mature projects to them before they consider spending further development money or making a production investment.

When a small to medium-sized project (ECU 1–5m) is launched into the marketplace for co-financing, a local broadcaster license fee deal is normally viewed as a critical lynchpin in that financial model. Indeed, UK producers have often found it particularly difficult to raise European finance without firstly having a UK broadcaster on board. TV money may not always come in the shape of straight development finance, but it plays a very important role in the financial packaging of projects in the market long before they get the green light and enter production.

New frequencies licensed by a range of European governments, and the proliferation of new technologies for transmission by satellite and cable, have meant the traditionally dominant public broadcasters across Europe have been challenged by a range of new channels in the past 4–5 years. One result is that there is a much larger demand for programming, including feature films.

Broadcasters' feature film strategies have responded to the new competitive market in a range of ways, including:

- Developing and making theatrical features, usually through a subsidiary company and normally through a co-financing/co-production venture rather than full equity financing.
- Developing and making movies for TV (outside this book's remit).
- Pre-buying and investing in films for theatrical release.

- Acquiring packages of films, now increasingly early and sometimes prior to a slate of films' production (e.g. Channel 4's pick up of the MK2-produced, Krzysztof Kieslowski-directed series, *Trois Couleurs*).

The key broadcasters, including the BBC, Channel 4, ZDF, RAI, RTVE, Canal Plus and TFI, tend not to develop projects themselves. Instead, they rely on a pool of ideas, treatments, scripts and projects from independent producers. If they do originate an idea, they will normally hire a writer/director and develop a script. Once the project is more developed, an independent producer will then take it into production. As noted above, Channel 4 and Le Studio Canal Plus are the key exceptions.

All broadcasters have certain schedules and audience demands to meet. Their film/drama operations fit into the larger requirements of the overall umbrella. They are aware of what films reach which audiences on television, and each broadcaster has carefully tailored 'taste' in terms of the kind of product they want to be associated with – and hence consider developing. Although considerably more secure financially than independent companies, broadcasters are often prepared to wait until a producer-writer-director team has developed a product to a reasonable level before making any financial commitment.

It should be noted that professionals stressed that feature film development has been heavily influenced by European broadcasters; specifically by the commissioning editor model. This model usually takes the following pattern: the idea is normally that of the writer, who is then left alone to write a draft. Minor modifications are then made before the project is shot for TV.

'That process has nothing to do with the process adopted by commercial film companies, which is much more akin to product development', explained David Puttnam. 'Each project is a product which is analysed, looked at from the point of view of the consumer and changed'.

The following section examines the key broadcasters in the main EU territories, and their policies towards feature film development.

4.1 DEVELOPMENT BY FRENCH BROADCASTERS

French broadcasters are legally obliged to invest certain minimum percentages of their annual turnover in feature film production. Of the main broadcasters, **Canal Plus** plays the largest role in film production.

The core business of Canal Plus is its pay-TV operation. The company is the most important player in the French film industry, and has expanded its service in a number of other territories, collaborating with local partners.

In addition to its feature film company, Le Studio Canal Plus, which has developed the Canal Plus Ecriture programme (see below for interview), the pay-TV operation is obliged under French law to acquire around 80–100 films per year. Including acquisition of pay-TV rights to the majority of these 100 films, Canal Plus estimates that it invests more than ECU 200m per annum in French cinema. Outside Le Studio, the pay-TV operation tends not to develop in-house material. It takes a stake in productions brought to the channel for co-financing under pay-TV license agreements. Most independent production development plans have a built-in slice of around 10% of a film's budget to be covered by a Canal Plus pick-up.

However, while this system looks enlightened as a production stimulus, producers privately conceded that 'basic scripts and subsequent development were often sub-standard' when brought to Canal Plus for investment. They contended that Canal Plus had to buy poor quality productions purely to fulfil its quota.

Didier Boujard, former director and founder of Canal Plus Ecriture, explains Ecriture's development strategy, while **Richard Grandpierre**, one of the two executives appointed in March 1995, adds his views on the operation.

> Canal Plus Ecriture's objective is to assist with first screenplays and films. We are here to nurture new potential talent, and by being behind them we hope to make younger and first-time film-makers more conscious of what they are doing. We provide the time and the means necessary for them to explore their ideas about story and character to the maximum.
>
> We are taking on around 15 script projects a year, of which we hope to have four or five worked into good completed scripts after 2 years or so. We are taking a long-term view and are allowing ourselves the luxury of some failures.
>
> The objective is not to be seen as a competitor to producers. We hope that our projects will be picked up by producers. The problem is that many French producers simply don't have the means to spend a long time on development, and certainly few have the financial means to take a significant risk on development.
>
> We finance the writers directly at present, although in the future we hope to re-sell the rights of the author to a producer for a sum covering at least the costs Ecriture incurred and up to the value of the completed screenplay. This is necessary if Ecriture is going to finance a lot of ideas and finish up with a handful of work.
>
> However, we are prepared to make deals where we will take an equivalent value through co-producing an Ecriture-backed film. Having taken a bet on a given risk, the idea is to follow this bet to its end. If we asked a producer to repay us when filming begins, this would probably mean that he would simply reduce what he spends on the overall film. Ecriture is prepared to defer repayment of our development investment. Each project costs varying amounts to develop.

We are working with writers, not teams, and because they are first feature films, option sales will be low. We start payments to writers as soon as they deliver their synopsis. We stay with them right through the development of the script, but we want to avoid artificially inflating the prices of first films. We have 25 contracted writers [in October 1994]; of those, seven have been abandoned, leaving 18 still in development. Although completed, scripts will be considered by Le Studio Canal Plus and the pay-TV buying operation, but nothing is automatically approved just because it has been developed by Ecriture.

Given the time needed for the development, production and commercial exploitation of a film, it will probably take Ecriture about 5 years of operation before we start to see returns in the system.

4.1.1 A NEW EXPANSION

Canal Plus Ecriture started a major new expansion in March 1995. A new brief was introduced that would allow the development initiative to find new writing and directing talent that has tended to be marginalized by the current French system of production finance and subsidy. The new version Canal Plus Ecriture will differ from its predecessor in terms of the range of projects and its ability to assist the development process far beyond just script re-writing. It will have a larger, undisclosed budget and will continue to work closely with the Equinox screenplay development programme.

The new development team is headed up by Nicholas Boukhrief and Richard Grandpierre. Boukhrief is a former editor of *Starfix* magazine and Canal Plus's *Journal Du Cinema*, and directed the feature *Va Mourire*. Grandpierre's background is in production, notably with Les Films De La Colline. He co-produced the hit comedy *La Vengeance d'une Blonde*. Former Ecriture head Didier Boujard moved across to Canal Plus's new multimedia division in March 1995.

The reason for the change appears to be due to the growing dissatisfaction at Canal Plus, particularly on the part of deputy managing director Alain de Greef, with current French films. They are neither adventurous nor spectacular enough for the broadcaster's requirements.

Grandpierre explains that 'The majority of French films we are obliged to buy have similar subjects, small theatrical audiences, and go on to attract a low number of viewers when we broadcast them. We will be looking to support films that have merits different to those sought by the CNC's Avances Sur Recettes, including, for example, projects that could have attracted Channel 4 or a producer like Roger Corman'.

Ecriture will 'where possible' try to break the author/director couplet, Grandpierre confirmed. 'That kind of film will be made in France anyway, and has no need for us. I think people are starting to understand that they need to work with other people and be open to criticism and suggestions. We are prepared to drop projects if someone becomes too demanding'.

TF1 Films Production was established in 1988, in the same year that the country's largest TV network was privatized. Like all other networks in France, TF1 has to meet certain minimum percentages or turnover that must be invested in cinema, making it the second largest film-backed channel in France after Canal Plus. In 1993, TF1 moved in the opposite direction from the public broadcasters, increasing its investment in co-productions from ECU 24.5 to 25.6m. This investment was spread across 19 feature films.

However, the key to TF1's co-production involvement in theatrical films has traditionally been one of predetermining which films will do best on French TV. This policy has significant ramifications. After pre-buying a large proportion of domestic feature comedies, it is now picking up TV rights for films produced by CiBy 2000, which is owned by the same group.

Overall, the role is less about early development or co-development, and more about cherry-picking projects that TF1 feel are suitable for transmission. TF1 managing director Guillaume de Verges is on record as saying: 'Producers need money, we need the films. There is no question of us touching the casting or scripts of films'.

4.2 DEVELOPMENT BY UK BROADCASTERS

The **BBC** overhauled its feature film operation in late 1993, with major ramifications for production and development finance. 'We do develop, but very sparingly. However, we do get scripts from independent producers that are in good shape, so there isn't always the need to hand over development money', said head of BBC Films Mark Shivas about his BBC Films department. Only material that is suitable for UK broadcasting transmission will be supported, with an understandable bias towards English-language and domestically-produced projects.

Between April 1994 and March 1995, Shivas' BBC Films spent ECU 240 000 on script and project development. For straight acquisitions (ECU 300 000 fees), development money will not come from the BBC, although Shivas will help find co-production partners. He is developing some of the films with ECU 900 000 BBC equity stakes. Although the BBC sees development primarily as 'script development' it does give 'modest amounts of money to producers primarily to help them go out to find other money'. Producer overheads are not covered, but smaller amounts are paid to producers, especially if they're working 'flat out to find co-finance'.

In addition to BBC Films, former British Screen staffer Tessa Ross was appointed in 1993 to commission independent producers. She has a development pool, of which about ECU 65 000 is expected to go towards feature film development. The money is there to help cover script writing, research, options, and a certain amount of independent overhead. She needs to place a developed project with the BBC – Shivas or a Screen One or Screen Two slot, the two key film/drama slots on the two BBC channels. The budget for these films is approximately ECU 1.7–4m.

Two TV film slots exist in the form of Screen One and Two, but neither of them is specifically designed for theatrical film development. Some may still be released in other territories through co-production partners, and exceptions, like Stephen Frears' *The Snapper* will win a release occasionally. However, the BBC announced in January 1995 that it will attempt to secure more theatrical releases for suitable product in development and work closely with The Sales Company, its sales agent, in marketing all its films.

Apart from France's Canal Plus, **Channel 4** is clearly Europe's most serious broadcasting source of finance for feature films. The channel spends ECU 18m per annum on features, with an average investment per film of around ECU 1–1.5m. The overall target is around 15 films per year, with budgets normally between ECU 1.3 and 6m.

Historically, Channel 4 has taken a very different approach to development when compared with the BBC (both past and present). Channel 4 had tended actively to develop a slate of films with independent producers. Once these screenplays had been developed, Channel 4 often discussed with British Screen which might be co-backed. This system is currently on hold due to a disagreement over British Screen's arrangement with BSkyB, which Channel 4 opposes.

Channel 4 develops in stages. The process starts with the script, then a budget and a schedule, followed by a second stage of development. On average there are four to five script drafts. Head of Channel 4's Drama department David Aukin suggested that their development pool has risen from ECU 450 000 in October 1990, to ECU 520 000 for 1992, to ECU 650 000 for 1993. For 1994 it went up to ECU 780 000 and in 1995/96 to ECU 1m. Even allowing for inflation, it is a significant trend. Consequently, it has more projects in development than nearly any UK-based producers. Channel 4 had around 43–44 projects in active development in 1994, and a similar figure by 1996.

Although development does not fall into 1 year periods, an approximate success ratio of developed project to production is around 1:3 (other sources put it at 1:4). Most importantly, 83% of all Channel 4 feature film productions have been developed by Aukin's department, a figure that has remained consistent for the last 3 years. (This trend is interesting, as it suggests again that producers are best off getting support for a project as early as possible from a key investor. Other producers have decried this, arguing that by going to a broadcaster so early, you invariably lose control of many of the rights.)

The average cost to Channel 4 for development per project is ECU 40 000, covering scripts, further and agreed development cost, and drafts. However, the company does not provide money for producers to enable them to go out to raise money elsewhere. 'We cannot support the overhead of production companies', stressed Aukin. 'I understand their problems, but there is no divine right to anything … It would be wonderful if schemes could be developed to help producers at the start of their careers. But if they don't have the ability to make things happen, they shouldn't be producing'.

'I do have to take a view when I put a film into development on whether it is a film that I am going to be able to help finance. I don't put films into development for the fun of it', said Aukin. He also has to take a view on a film's budget, which effectively means that he has to make sure that it fits into his overall limits.

However, Channel 4 has proved highly flexible in the later stages of development, showing a willingness to advance monies to support a production in pre-production if the broadcaster is committed to producing the film. These monies are used to support location scouting and casting, and other costs incurred in late-development/early pre-production.

Since the new **ITV** network system was implemented in 1993, the Network Centre has decided not to acquire license fees for UK feature films and has no interest in 'foreign language' films. Network head Marcus Plantin is focussing on the schedule rather than one-offs, although companies like Granada hope to persuade him that feature product could play an important role in his schedule. By the end of 1995, they had not managed to make any impact on his initial reticence. The result is a significant drop in feature film development and production.

The only ITV company now continuing to develop features with any serious degree of commitment is **Granada Film**. It is doing so knowing that it cannot at present sell its features to the Network Centre and acquire license fee funding (around ECU 700 000 per film). Granada had eight films in development in 1994, spending ECU 240 000 on these projects during that period. Granada Film plans to make three to four films over the next 3 years. The company has only gone into production twice since 1991, with *Jack and Sarah* and *August*, the first films since *The Field*.

4.3 DEVELOPMENT BY GERMAN BROADCASTERS

Overall, TV's role in German film production is clearly important. In 1994, about 40% of the territory's domestic film productions were made as co-productions with the public broadcasters. However, relations between German TV and film-makers have long been fraught. Heinz Ungureit, ZDF's director of European Co-operation, held forth at the 1994 Berlin Film Festival about the difficulties of reconciling German film subsidies with TV support.

Dr Ungureit pointed out that TV was constantly having to listen to the old reproach that television executives 'always spoil the wonderful feature films which would fill the big screen with all sorts of lovely things if the terrible TV people didn't get in the way, and bring it down to the scale of a small TV play'. However, he added that 'when fiction editors did try to warn producers away from making a theatrical film on serious creative grounds, producers would counter that they already had funding from various subsidy boards, and were not prepared to give this financing up'.

Although not strictly financing development, ZDF's role as a potential buyer should not be underestimated in the development process. 'In 70% or 80% of cases, we warn producers, saying that in our opinion their project is not a cinema film, and that they should look for another story or make this one larger and different', said Ungureit.

ZDF's future policy is likely to move more towards the BBC and Channel 4 approach, which both support films for mostly cultural reasons. 'We believe that this form of film-making is most at risk. We must see that the existing talent, the real film-makers, authors, directors, are put in the position where they can make films'.

German public broadcasters **ARD** and **ZDF** have a 30-year tradition of supporting domestic film production through co-production. Many directors of the New German Cinema, including Fassbinder, Schloendorff, Wenders and Herzog, worked closely with the public broadcasters, sometimes on TV films, and sometimes on feature films that also had theatrical runs.

In 1974, the TV/film relationship was formalized with the signing of a 'Film/Television Agreement' which required ARD and ZDF to commit funds annually for co-productions, and to allow the resulting films a minimum 2-year window before playing in their schedules. Around ECU 130m has been provided to more than 400 feature film productions under the Agreement. In the latest extension of the Agreement, signed in April 1993 by ZDF, ARD and the Federal Film Board (FFA), the two broadcasters committed to paying an annual ECU 7.4m between 1993 and 1995 for co-productions 'which will enrich programmes of the cinema and the television schedules, thereby also strengthening the film industry as a whole'.

A further ECU 5.7m each year is being channelled into the FFA's 'project assistance fund', which has so far backed films like *The House of the Spirits*, *Stalingrad*, *Go Trabi Go* and *Asterix in America*. However, this money is normally put into production, not development. Finally, a ECU 1.5m pot is being allocated through to 1995 for 'newcomers' and first-time film-makers. Previous beneficiaries include Jaco van Dormael (*Toto the Hero*) and Nico Hoffman (*November*).

ZDF's film wing, Kleines Fernsehspiel, initially backed short films in the 1960s, but has concentrated on experimental/avant garde niche film-makers such as Derek Jarman, Jim Jarmusch, Theo Angelopoulos and Fassbinder among others. The section is run by Eckart Stein, and has about ECU 4–5m for programming between 30 and 40 slots a year. The spread leads to a low level of finance per film and low-budget productions. Crucially, Stein's editorial team have developed very personal links with film-makers, many whom have started their careers and developed them thanks to the department. Although there is a very limited specific development money available, ZDF has a significant role in advising what kind of films in development it is likely to ultimately support. However, the film wing is currently under review, and faces an uncertain future.

4.4   DEVELOPMENT BY SPANISH BROADCASTERS

Spain's public broadcaster **RTVE** has invested advance rights money in 100 of the 521 Spanish films produced from 1985 to 1991. Although picking up early transmission rights is not strictly 'development' finance, it has a considerable 'financial engineering' role in the process of pushing a project towards production, and should be taken into consideration in the development process.

RTVE's average investment in each individual film normally amounts to around 30% of the total film budget. However, RTVE suffered from a major financial crisis in 1991/92, which was reflected in its acquisitions policy. The broadcasters' investment peak was in 1988, when it bought rights to 28 films, and it dropped to an all-time low in 1992 when no investment was made.

In 1991 RTVE signed thirteen rights contracts with film producers, for a total of approximately ECU 7m. Following no investment in 1992, in 1993 it signed four contracts worth just one quarter of its 1991 investment. RTVE's estimated investment for 1994 is a more healthy total of ECU 6.8m with, to date, contracts signed for six films.

Most encouraging for the Spanish feature production sector is the recent agreement signed between RTVE and FAPAE, the Spanish Federation of Producers. The deal involves a commitment by RTVE to invest up to ECU 13m from 1995 to 1998 inclusive. RTVE will take early pick-up transmission rights for feature films produced by members of the FAPAE. The agreement also involves the Official Credit Institute, which will facilitate soft credit lines to producers for the production of films picked up by RTVE. The deal is seen as marking a return of RTVE to its former days of strong investment in Spanish film production.

Antena 3 Television, the private Spanish television channel, has recently launched a new film arm with major national and international partners. Aurum Films was announced at the 1994 MIFED market. Although essentially a sales and distribution arm, the new company also provides advance financing on Spanish co-productions. Aurum Films has six to nine production partnerships with Spanish companies, all scheduled to shoot in 1995. It has also acquired slates from New Line Cinema, Rysher Entertainment, Trimark Pictures, Island World and PolyGram Filmed Entertainment.

Most important from a development point of view, Antena 3 Television has entered into a domestic production alliance with three of Spain's major companies: CARTEL, Origen and Atrium Productions. Under an umbrella title, Leader Films, the three companies plan to create a product development department with each of the partners investing ECU 18 000–24 000. The idea behind the corporate alliance is for the three partners to have more clout in all areas from development and production, to sales and distribution.

4.5 DEVELOPMENT BY ITALIAN BROADCASTERS

A severe drop in advertising revenue in 1993 and 1994 has caused Italy's public broadcaster **RAI-Television** (and the main private network, Fininvest, see below) to make sweeping cuts in their 1993 and 1994 film production and acquisition budgets. This important trend is probably behind the overall steep decline in Italian film production from 1992 (127) and 1993 (106). Only 86 films were 100% Italian-financed in 1993, compared with 114 the previous year.

Over the past 10 years, Italian producers have come to depend on pre- or post-production funding, very small amounts of seed money for development and start-up capital from television to help put together financial packages. Making a film without the near-certainty of selling Italian TV rights to RAI or Fininvest is considered financial suicide without a strong co-financier/producer or the likelihood of foreign sales.

RAI used to make extensive use of a process called 'contract activation' or 'a contract bridge'. At the discretion of the network head, RAI would put up a reasonable amount of money for a producer to use for the development of a film project, covering 50% of the acquisition of rights, script development, budget preparation and location scouting. If one withdrew, the other partner could go ahead with the film. Politically attacked as open to abuse and favouritism, the practice has been pushed right back to maybe one in five projects, according to RAI-3 producer Gabriella Carosio. Altogether, RAI never puts up more than 33% of a film's budget.

RAI is in the middle of a financial and political crisis. A new 'macro structure' is being created to centralize film and fiction production and acquisitions by RAI's three networks. It is too early to be clear about budget levels for development, let alone the overall investment level in feature production.

Fininvest, Italy's main private broadcasting operation, used to provide development finance in two ways. Either the film was a Penta production or co-production, in which case partner Berlusconi would provide most of the budget upfront, or it was pre-sold to his Fininvest TV networks through his software division.

According to Giuseppe Cereda, who ran film production at Silvio

Berlusconi Communications (SBC) until 1994, SBC co-produced some 20 films from 1991 to 1993. In 3 years of activity, Cereda said he didn't commission any single scripts. 'We conducted our work from scripts submitted to us by directors and producers, deciding whether to enter into the project'.

SBC announced in early 1994 that it will cut back on feature film acquisitions for TV by a sizeable 50%, while its TV production budget is being cut by 20%, to around $30m. Fininvest's future is also unclear since Silvio Berlusconi moved into and then out of politics.

KEY SUMMARY POINTS

1. A distinction needs to be made between broadcasters which have feature wings, and support feature film development with a view to investing more than just a license fee in the product; and broadcasters who simply pick up film rights before or after the product has been completed.
2. Broadcasters' development pattern for television drama has not necessarily helped feature film development strategy. Professionals stressed that feature film development has been heavily influenced by European broadcasters; specifically by the commissioning editor model. This model usually takes the following pattern: the idea is normally the writer's, who is then left alone to write a draft. Minor modifications are then made before the project is shot for TV. The process is very different to fully-fledged feature film development.
3. Public broadcasters are currently facing a considerable crisis due to the uncertainty of their traditional funding sources through the public purse. Rising production costs and growing competition have put pressure on many of them to cut back. Film development and equity investments in productions have been affected, although not as much as other areas. Film remains a prestige area for broadcasters to be attached to, hence the BBC, Channel 4, Canal Plus and RTVE, for example, have all ensured the continued funding of constructive film policies. When ZDF considered cutting back on its film wing, Kleines Fernsehspiel, the move was met by considerable public criticism.
4. Private broadcasters are only recently starting to make an impact on film development and production. High start-up costs and the ability to buy films at a lower premium compared to making their own production investments have tended to keep private broadcasters away from development and production. However, Spain's Antena 3 and the UK-based BSkyB are interesting indications of how new sources of production funding for producers will gradually become available.

Privately-funded film companies 5

For any major company with a regular output of feature film product, development is invariably viewed as a cost within the overall business plan. A portion of this cost is normally allocated as an above-the-line sum to each film produced; which in most cases should lead to a project's development costs being paid back on first day of production. Projects that are developed but fail to go into production are written off.

However, each company has a high degree of latitude in terms of:

- The precise timing of when to decide a project is no longer 'alive'.
- The financial strength to negotiate new options on material.
- How much of the total 'overhead' is in part paid for within the production budget of each film, including development costs.

The following section concentrates on the activities of PolyGram Filmed Entertainment (PFE), as a case study of how a large company approaches development.

Other companies' strategies, including Gaumont, UGC, Studio Babelsberg, Ufa, Canal Plus, Chargeurs, CiBy 2000, Hachette, CineVox and other, large independent producers, are detailed later in this chapter (contact details are in the Directory of Contacts). However, it should be made clear that many of the companies contacted were unwilling to reveal accurate, precise data about the levels of money spent on development. Success ratios of development-to-production levels are also almost impossible to establish beyond informed estimates. This is partly related to the lengthy, drawn-out process of developing film projects. Some projects are 'in development' for more than 5 years before reaching the camera.

The larger company research indicates (through interviews rather than hard figures) that the ratio of projects developed to films produced is still very high when compared to Hollywood's average studio ratio of around one project made for every 20 developed (high means two to three projects developed or less per film made; an estimated average ratio for the large independent producers is one film made for every four developed). Importantly, the research also demonstrates that national trends and domestic approaches to development tend to be replicated by the larger independents, but companies are more 'studio-like' in their approach; notably Polygram Filmed Entertainment (PFE).

5.1   CASE STUDY: POLYGRAM FILMED ENTERTAINMENT

PolyGram is the closest European-based operation to a US studio, although there are significant differences (in addition to its European interests, PFE also owns stakes in US-based companies, including Propaganda, 51% of Interscope and distributor Gramercy).

Since the Dutch-owned company announced its ECU 230m investment in film in 1992, it has set up centres of production talent on a similar basis to its music label system. The ultimate aim is to create a mini-major film studio with strong feeds from both US and European partners or part-owned/fully owned subsidiaries. PFE took a 100% stake in UK production outfit Working Title in 1992 and 51% of French company Cinea in 1993. It bought Movies Film Productions, one of Holland's leading production and distribution outfits in March 1994. This new Dutch company is now called PolyGram Filmed Entertainment BV and its production arm Movies Film Productions has become Meteor Film Productions. It now produces approximately one English-language and one Dutch-language film per year.

PolyGram has a development pool for each subsidiary. Each 'label' applies annually for resources (general overhead, development and production funds) in late September for the following year. Once that sum is allocated, each production subsidiary is free to decide how to invest the money.

The following case study examines how UK production satellite Working Title develops material, followed by an interview with Stewart Till, president of PFE International.

According to **Working Title**'s co-head Eric Fellner, 'We can spend the money for development in whatever way we want. If we want a large sum of money to be in the market to buy ECU 1m books' rights, we would apply for much more than if we just wanted to develop internal material'.

Working Title, under the PFE umbrella, had only been operating fully for 18 months at the time of interview, so reliable ratios were impossible. However, Fellner says that successful development depends on the kind of genre being developed: 'On some projects it is 2–3:1; on others it is 10:1. If it is a mainstream project and we are spending a lot of money on its development, then the ratio comes right down'. The theory is that Working Title will make three to four films a year in the ECU 13–18m range – although some are bigger – and 'we will probably develop at any one time some 20 to 30 "live" projects', said Fellner.

No overall development figure per annum was forthcoming, but according to other sources close to the company, Working Title has at least ECU 1.14m a year for development purposes. Fellner suggested that they had spent 'at least ECU 570 000 on development' during the 18 months since PolyGram bought the company.

Working Title uses UK directors for around 70–80% of its projects and 50% UK writers, 'but we would like to use more. We definitely have a bias towards wanting to make UK/European projects, but we are in the business of feeding a distribution system. We have to look for films on which we can get a positive return. We are not in the market to make esoteric arthouse films, but we are still in the market to make interesting European films', said Fellner.

A key point in this case study 'programme' should be stressed, because other larger companies also mentioned it during the research. Although PFE is one of Europe's largest production combines, when production is delegated to smaller, albeit well-financed entities, there is a limit to how many projects can be maintained at full-development stage.

The level of work required to convert a developing project into production is very high. Slates of 30 films mean that only five or six are really on the 'front burner' for conversion at any one time. In other words, only around 25% of a company's 'slate' is actually undergoing fully-fledged development at any one time. Once again, professionals interviewed emphasized that what mattered was the 'quality' of the development strategy, rather than the 'quantity' of projects on a slate.

PFE's president **Stewart Till** explains the company's development strategy:

In 2–3 years' time, PolyGram will be operating as a studio. What that will mean is the production of around 15–20 Hollywood films, with average budgets of around $20–25m, with one or two films in the $50m budget-plus category.

Unlike Hollywood, we will be supporting that slate with local language productions from all the countries where we have our own distribution outlets. One to two films a year per country will be produced at appropriate budget levels. At the moment we are in eight of the 12 major territories around the world (including the UK, France, North America, Benelux, Australia, Canada, Hong Kong and Spain). We are deliberately building them one by one, so that we get them right. Once we've bedded them down, we will move onto the next one.

An awful lot of development money is wasted. Some of the US studios spend astronomical sums on it, and 'development hell' is a very expensive area. To avoid overspending, you have to get the levels right. That means not being wasteful, but giving the film the right shot. But that's tough, because on the other hand, you almost cannot spend too much money on development. Our green-light system operates by letting the producing units come up with projects. They then present them in the form of a script, potential cast and director and a proper budget. We don't just have production companies approaching executives saying: 'Hey, isn't this a great script, let's do it'. We do try to make the process as empirical and as rational as possible.

Specifically, various parts of PFE do revenue projections on proposed projects from our different outlets. PolyGram Film International (PFI, formerly Manifesto Film Sales) will do the foreign sales projections; our own distributors will have an input on their territories; although PFI has the final say. The US arms do theatrical, television and video projections. Simplistically, if the revenue exceeds the costs of the film and there is cash available and allocated for that year from the production budget, we will do it.

The advantage of the label system of different production outlets is that no one person at the top is dealing with so many projects that they can't see the wood for the trees. The guy with the green light may not see material three levels down. Whereas people at the top of our different companies know all their projects intimately.

Having said that, it is not really possible for a film to be given the green light without PFE's top management, Michael Kuhn, Alain Levy and myself. And Kuhn has the ability to greenlight the odd project that doesn't necessarily add up. PolyGram does not meddle creatively. The top management may say that a project doesn't work because we cannot get the pre-sales with the suggested cast, but we don't meddle or try to fix it, because that's not our area of expertise.

There have been weaknesses with our systems on occasion. For example, when Working Title started, we undoubtedly put some projects into production before they were ready. We also spent so much on certain projects' development, that the temptation was to say: 'We've spent ECU 650 000, so we have to go into production'. That is totally wrong too. It's no good spending good money after bad. However wonderful projects are, the 'go' rate is always less than you may think it should be. If all 10 projects look fabulous, with the best will in the world, not more than two should get away into production.

Overall, our production style will hopefully offer more value for money than the studios, in that we have that independent-like concern over the pennies that the studios don't have. There is no set style, which is very deliberate and explains why we have so many different production companies. PolyGram has the attitude of an independent but the muscle of a major studio.

appointment in June 1994 of experienced producer Timothy Burrill to head Chargeurs Productions Ltd in London. The appointment was made by Chargeurs chief Jerome Seydoux, with an expressed interest in finding strong English language projects to help fill AMLF and Guild's distribution line-ups.

'All options are open', explained Burrill. 'I am chasing respected and established British and Irish directors, many of whom have made films in Hollywood recently, with a view to finding a strong project they could make in Europe. I am not interested in heavily North American or Hollywood projects. On the development side, I have the ability to pick up options on books with a high potential for adaptation, develop them with established writers, and then offer them to directors. I read all scripts myself, but they are all solicited from writers and directors I know. Ultimately, any material I really like is recommended to Jerome [Seydoux] in Paris'.

RCS Films & Television

A company that has a strong interest in video and film distribution, RCS Films & TV looked set to enter the film development aspect of its business in a unique way. In association with its UK fully-owned subsidiary Majestic Films and TV, the company was set to pay for all the development costs on 15 international film projects in 1994/95. This A-range development slate strategy hit problems in 1994 with the unravelling of the Ridley and Tony Scott relationship, and the resignation of RCS Film and Television chief Paolo Glisenti in September 1994.

On the development front, 'no monetary figure has been set', said acquisitions executive Gianmaria Dona delle Rose. 'That will depend on how far we agree to carry each developed project forward – from just buying the option, to full development and a complete script for shooting'. In exchange for their investment, RCS/Majestic will take all foreign (non-North American) distribution rights. The development slate is designed to ensure that Majestic has at least nine films a year to distribute.

Studio Babelsberg

Nearly 600 treatments and scripts are being looked at per year by the relatively new studio based at the former DEFA site in Potsdam. Around 10–15 projects make the final selection for development and potential production slate. Head of development Thomas Bavermeister selects with his two development colleagues through a consultation process with 'practitioners', by which he means distributors and producers in the main.

Studio joint-chief Volker Schloendorff has a very specific approach to development (dubbed the 'Schloendorff concept'). This involves the director's input in the development 'team' process, and the testing of the project with distributors, often through short pitching meetings.

'If resistance is very hard, then you learn that maybe you have to re-examine your project', said Schloendorff. 'There has to be a certain focus to the whole thing, with a team put together, not just a writer'. Babelsberg has set up as a 'mediator', a key contact point for independents and writers, who often have potential ideas but do not have the financial or structural means of taking them further. Former DEFA directors/writers are also being encouraged to submit projects.

UFA/Babelsberg

Owned by German media giant Bertelsmann, UFA has funded a development slate out of its own private funds up to now. It took an office on the Babelsberg Studio site in Potsdam in 1993.

According to the Treuhand contract (privatization agency) with CGE (now owner of Babelsberg Film Studios), 10% of the overall production budget of ECU 31m over 4 years must be invested in development. That means an investment of around ECU 780 000 per annum, although UFA executive Dr Gabriella Pfandner stressed that this figure is theoretical as the development level will depend on what projects are submitted for consideration. UFA Babelsberg currently has around 10 projects in development.

Nordisk Film

This major Danish (and key Scandinavian) company is involved in about 65% of Danish feature film production, and has extensive distribution and exhibition interests. In the 1980s a change of policy was implemented. Instead of concentrating on one or two productions a year, it now spreads its investment into six, usually in partnership with smaller independent producers and co-financiers.

Over the past 5 years, the company has had around 10–12 projects in development per year. About 50% of these are abandoned, 'mostly when the Danish Film Institute decides not to award a production subsidy', said Nordisk executive and main producer, Lars Kolvig. 'We see Nordisk as a finance centre, trying to open gates for new people with new ideas'. Kolvig estimates that he receives some 50–80 scripts a year, of which perhaps one or two are used; the rest are developed in-house.

The range of spending on development starts at around ECU 4600 up to a fully-fledged developed project at ECU 130 000. Although Kolvig is basically satisfied with the system, he would prefer to have a proper development department, but said that the cost would be too high. 'Undoubtedly too many projects are brought to production too early', he conceded. 'We haven't the time to give them one more turn. Today we do try to be more careful'.

Sogetel

In 1994, the Spanish-based production company Sogetel, the film production arm of multimedia group PRISA, reached a joint venture agreement with Spanish producer Andrés Vicente Gómez (representing Iberoamericana and Lola Films) to produce a film slate of eight to 10 films annually, to 1997.

An initial fund of ECU 300 000 has been established to devote to development with the Sogetel/Iberoamericana projected film slate. The strategy is to develop some 60–70 projects over the next 3 years, of which up to 30 would actually be produced. The development fund is conceived as a revolving fund, with a percentage of box-office returns on the films produced going back into the fund. Sogetel will maintain a minimum equity stake of 51% in all of the films encompassed in the agreement, as well as controlling the financial management of the productions.

Gómez will act as executive producer on all the projects approved by a central development board comprised of representatives from all the parties concerned. Gómez will not be producing any films outside this deal during the 3-year period. The estimated production slate is expected to attract an investment of more than ECU 50m.

5.3.2   MEDIUM-SIZED INDEPENDENT COMPANIES

CineVox

According to chief executive Dieter Geissler, CineVox has an in-house, revolving development fund of ECU 1.1m. Geissler anticipates that CineVox's share of development costs will be between ECU 130 000–260 000 per project. 'We are often co-developing with partners, and are investing totals of up to ECU 1m per project through to pre-production, i.e. until all expected collaterals, subsidies and the completion bond is in place, and the project goes into full production', explained Geissler.

CineVox has only started developing a slate of projects since 1992. Geissler expects the ratio of pictures being finally produced from this slate to be one out of three. Costs per project have risen due to CineVox paying higher writers' fees.

Neue Constantin Films

Bernd Eichinger's production and distribution outfit bankrolls all its own development costs, which he estimates amount to around $2m per year. The level of development normally comes to around 10–20% of the production's final budget. Of the projects developed, 70%, or approximately two out of three, goes into production. Eichinger does work closely with smaller independents.

For example, in 1992 Neue Constantin signed a 3-year contract with smaller independent company Sonke Wortman to develop feature projects after the success of the company's 1991 TV film, *Allein Unter Frauen*. Eichinger expanded on his views on and approach towards development in Cannes 1994, during the European Film College's Ebeltoft lecture. 'Having the money for development is vital for any producer who wants his movies to get made and to make money. I have always taken care to have enough money to develop everything out of my own pocket. If you are not able to do that, you'll soon find yourself in a very bad position regarding the people who control the development process'.

Eichinger is open to smaller independents bringing strong commercial projects to him. For example, UK producer Jeremy Bolt and director Paul Anderson are set to make the $40m sci-fi project *The Stars My Destination* with Constantin Films. Eichinger had been developing Alfred Bester's story, and was keen to work with Anderson and Bolt on the project.

Enigma Productions

David Puttnam's UK-based production company spends about ECU 650 000 per year on book options, screenplays, writers' fees and expenses related to development. Enigma spends around ECU 160 000 in developing each project (with budgets ranging from ECU 6 to 35m). Through the company's relationship with Warner Bros, a development 'pool' has been nearly fully-financed by the Studio. In return, it has First Look – not an Output – deal and Puttnam has the right to move the project forward independently if they reject it.

By the end of 1993, Enigma had three films in development, one in pre-production, one in post-production and one completed. When asked about success ratios, Puttnam pointed out that there is no 'end-date' to a developed project having to go into production, although on average it abandons one project per year. Over a 5-year period (1988–1993), the company has produced seven features, four of which went theatrical and three of which went to cable.

Puttnam stressed that the company goes through on average seven or eight drafts of a script, and sometimes many more, while 'most films in

Europe go through two drafts'. Enigma recently entered production on a film it has been developing for 5 years, underlining the inexactness of ratios and the length of time that money is risked in the development process.

Filmauro

Like other Italian film companies, Filmauro is unable to pinpoint a specific investment figure as regards development finance. This is a revealing trend. Film development throughout Italy is an acutely inexact science. 'We have no budget for development', explained Filmauro company executive Maurizio Amati. 'We put up money on a project-by-project basis'.

For an Italian or European film, development costs can range from a minimum of ECU 26 500 through to ECU 50 000–80 000. 'There is no standard', explained Filmauro producer Aurelio De Laurentiis, who developed seven to eight projects in 1994, of which about five will probably go into production. Amati suggests that '90% of their projects become completed films'. He pointed out (as did many people interviewed in different territories for this book), that the Italian industry is different in structure to the American system and hence does not devote time and money to film development in the same way, or with the same volume of investment.

Recorded Picture Company

Jeremy Thomas' UK-based production company has produced four films over the last 5 years, and developed around eight. Production budgets range from around ECU 20 to 40m. According to RPC's managing director Chris Auty, the company has 'a very high success rate on projects developed, because we only ever develop projects with directors attached. For us, the director is the beginning, middle and the end of the equation. We do not buy a literary property and develop a script. Either a director has a pet project or comes to us and says they want to work with us. The central figure who is going to make the films is on board from the beginning'.

RPC's development costs vary enormously and depend largely on the director and the scale of the film. Bertolucci's *Little Buddha* was understood to have cost more than ECU 260 000 to develop, while on the smaller scale, RPC have a project in development with Angelica Huston called *Terrible Beauty* – about Irish poet W.B. Yeat's muse Maud Gonne. The development stage is being supported by SCRIPT and British Screen. However, the amounts loaned by these two sources are relatively small – ECU 26 000– 60 000 – compared to what RPC would expect to spend in total, which may go as high as 5% of the eventual budget. The company is currently in the middle of a development deal with UGC.

Chrysalis Group

In September 1994, Chrysalis Group PLC, the media and entertainment group, set up Chrysalis Films. The publicly quoted company committed itself to fund up to ECU 5.2m over 4 years to a series of First Look development and overheads deals with comedy film-maker John Goldstone and two up-coming British producers, Gary Sinyor and Richard Holmes.

Early in 1995, Chrysalis also moved to acquire 100% of Red Rooster Film & TV, run by Linda James and Stephen Bayly. It has also acquired a substantial shareholding in Nik Powell and Stephen Woolley's Scala Productions. Lyndsey Posner has been brought in from media law firm Simon Olswang & Co. to run the new film division.

'We decided to set up this development fund because there is a limited amount of talent around and very few people are prepared to do what we are doing', said Mick Pilsworth, chief executive of Chrysalis Visual Entertainment. 'It is a relatively low-cost method of getting into the marketplace'.

Chrysalis Films is not aiming to finance production but it may provide gap financing. 'In addition, we should be able to help our producers obtain production finance because of our stronger commercial position in the marketplace', notes Pilsworth. Chrysalis picked the young producers because, says Pilsworth, they are commercial and they have all made one film. At the moment, Chrysalis Films does not plan to make new development deals, although this strategy may change, depending on whether the existing deals yield enough product.

5.3.3   THE SMALLER INDEPENDENT COMPANIES

The majority of smaller independent production companies across the whole of Europe are driven towards production as quickly as possible, and with as many of their projects as possible. Why? Without proper capitalization, an independent company investing in feature films survives mainly from earning money when in production. The amounts spent on development within the majority of medium and smaller companies have depended heavily on available funds: primarily past profits and ownership of rights which can be mortgaged, or direct development subsidies.

Part of the problem independent companies face is the lack of networking between them. Former SCRIPT director general Bo Christensen pointed out that, 'independent companies rarely meet each other across Europe on a regular basis. They need to network and build projects at the development stage where possible. It is clear that smaller companies are not working at the same consistent level as the larger ones'.

Most companies interviewed for this section stressed how precarious and inconsistent these key elements are. Some smaller companies which exist in territories where development finance is very limited have traditionally raised development finance from banks, usually at steep interest rates (e.g. Italy). The genuinely small companies struggle to raise a low-interest loan from the Banca Nazionale del Lavoro's Sezione Autonoma Credito Cinematografico (SACC). More commercially orientated (medium-sized) companies have given up trying to qualify for these loans. They have resorted to regular bank credit at interest rates topping 22%.

Where there are few development funds available (e.g. Spain/Portugal, where little public or private finance is readily available), the development financier is in reality the screenplay writer, who either defers payment or is simply not paid for his/her work. This deferment in payment, nonetheless, means that the producer has the script to work with and hence can still generate development on the project.

In Spain, the research showed that around 10–17% of annual turnover was spent on development by both big and small companies. More revealing in terms of fragmentation, a 1993 survey of Spanish production shows that 40 producers only produced one film, 10 producers made two films and five producers participated in three or more projects.

Between 1987 and 1993, Irish producers had no real domestic support for development (or production). During that time, a considerable number applied for and were awarded development loans from SCRIPT. However, in addition to this, small companies also applied to SCALE and CARTOON for development support. Rather than trying to raise development finance privately from domestic sources, most concentrated on looking to European sources of finance and development support.

Although Scandinavia has a well-organized subsidy structure, including development funds, one interesting example of smaller independent companies being 'lifted up' by collaborating with the largest production houses was uncovered in Denmark. Most of the eight or nine smaller members of Danish Association of feature film producers are increasingly collaborating with the 'big two', Nordisk and Metronome. The relationships are specifically focussed on development as well as production support, with the major companies helping the independents pay for strong scripts and moving them into pre-production. One independent, Regner Grasten, has recently firmly attached himself to Nordisk, and has broken new ground by hiring three salaried, full-time scriptwriters to work on his latest projects (*Vildbassin* and *Kun En Pige*).

However, key Danish independent producers, such as Nina Crone, pointed out that the smaller companies are still heavily dependent on 'subsidies, subsidies, subsidies'. Access to development finance has become more difficult in Norway for small producers. John Jacobsen's Filmkemeratene suggested that film development in the independent sector is done 'without any money at all', and that most producers have to concentrate on one good idea and make that go into production.

Smaller French independent companies tend still to push the auteur/

director-driven model, rather than invest in fully-fledged development. A treatment/script is seen as part of the director's responsibility, rather than an element that has to be worked on within a development team. This creates serious problems, as specialist writers (i.e. non-directors) are invariably undervalued in France.

In addition, it should be noted that interviewees pointed out that certain types of subsidy systems have a direct influence over pushing production companies towards a green-light rather than further development. A brief example is the French 'compte de soutien' – an automatic subsidy earned in proportion to the success of previous productions. Even companies which have been allocated production support from the above, or the 'Avances Sur Recettes', often find themselves unable to fully develop their projects as these subsidies can only be accessed when they start production and not before.

German independent producers and writers have been spoilt by extensive funds for development and scriptwriting, said interviewees. However, the emphasis has tended to be skewed by selection committees who seem more interested in the literary qualities of the work than its potential for the market. According to one medium-sized producer, the ratios he's worked with are as follows: From treatment to production: 1:5; where a script is written: 1:3; and where the writer has worked by themselves: 1:10 or worse.

These figures are similar to SCRIPT's problems with single writer loans, where none of the single writer projects have gone into production to date. However, most German independents conceded that not enough time has been given to the development and preparation of films. The level of criticism has been so high and public, that many producers felt that the public funding systems were starting to take note.

The majority of the UK's smaller independent companies are tied into the low-budget, broadcasters' model. Public sources of development finance (British Screen, Scottish Film Production Fund, etc.) and Broadcasters (Channel 4, BBC, Granada) are servicing a specific budget area: up to ECU 4m. The typical range is ECU 1.3–2.8m.

Although there is a lot of talk about larger production companies providing development cash (Working Title, Portman/Zenith, Red Rooster, Chrysalis, etc.), there was little evidence uncovered by the UK research (Table 4) that demonstrated that genuinely smaller independent producers as a group have access to them. The overall tendency suggested that larger companies tend to work on their own material, with their own established writers, and with their own development agendas.

KEY SUMMARY POINTS

Traditionally, First Look deals with (mainly) US partners have not been common in Europe. However, there is a generally acknowledged shortage

Table 4 UK producers' development records (1989–1993)

Producers	Projects in development 5 years	Projects in development per annum	Development budgets average/MAX (£)	Development budgets/TOTA per annum (£)	No. of productions/ 5 years	No. of productions 1993	No. of productions 1994
Large producers							
Enigma, David Puttnam	12	3	125 000.00	500 000.00	7	2	2
Scala/Palace	18	7	125 000.00		14	1	2
Recorded Picture Co.	8	4	175 000.00		4	1	3
Working Title	65	30			15	2	2
Zenith		10	30 000.00	150 000.00	7	2	2
Simon Relph		6	60 000.00		9	2	3
Medium							
Parallax	14	8	35 000.00	15 000.00	4	2	3
Sarah Radclyffe					4	2	2
Simon Channing Williams							
Thin Man Films	5				5	0	0
Small							
Richard Holmes	5	4			1	0	1
Jenny Howarth	5	3	20 000.00		3	1	
Lynda Myles		5	60 000.00		2	1	0
Alison Owen					2	1	2
Simon Channing Williams							
Image Productions	10				1	1	
Totals	142				78	18	22

of strong product both in the US, Europe and around the international market. Hence distributors are tending to chase a limited amount of suitable films in the market at any one time. The resulting strategy in reaction to this shortage is for financiers/buyers/distributors to tie up rights early.

However, if these kinds of deals are expected to grow in number, will they have a direct bearing on the type of product developed? Some argue they will, leading European producers towards more mainstream, commercially-driven product (see PolyGram's comments above.)

Their great advantage is in the encouragement of vertical integration: the linking of production and distribution. Development is a high-risk area of investment. The more a company or producer can cover that risk by providing committed outlets for their product, the stronger their business plan will be.

These deals help cement relationships between the development/ production area and the distributor/end-user. They help combat the current fragmentation European developers/producers suffer from heavily. Major producers suggested for this research that if a company can find someone to develop a script/slate with them, who also has the capacity to subsequently finance their film(s), then it is better off going with that system.

Pan-European funds and initiatives

6

6.1 INTRODUCTION TO THE MEDIA PROGRAMME

The EC has implemented an ambitious programme for Europe's audiovisual industry, first through a pilot phase from 1986 to 1990, and then through the first 5-year MEDIA Programme, which was completed at the end of 1995. Described as 'an economic support mechanism for cultural activities', MEDIA's system is not based on a straight, non-returnable subsidy. Instead, the majority of its working practices are conducted through seed capital, which tends to be soft-loaned by most MEDIA projects.

Of the MEDIA I Programme's different initiatives, the European Script Fund (SCRIPT) was the one most specifically focused on development. This chapter examines SCRIPT's history and practice, and then examines other MEDIA initiatives, such as the Media Business School (MBS), ACE and SOURCES, followed by other non-MEDIA development initiatives.

6.2 THE EUROPEAN SCRIPT FUND (SCRIPT)

Talk of a European Script Fund during the mid-1980s gave rise to a range of ideas about what development for film and television fiction really was. Officials across Europe privately commented that they had a vague notion of what SCRIPT was intended to achieve, 'but no real idea of what development actually meant'. Other senior film figures at the early stage of SCRIPT's birth were obsessed with the idea of supporting writers and screenplays. However, many of them did not attempt to draw a connection between the writing process and the broader demands of the development process, including marketing and fund-raising.

SCRIPT's strategy was to act as an incentive for writers, producers and directors to further their ideas, preferably with other European partners, and ultimately push them towards production – a kind of development partnership role rather than an administrative soft hand-out. Loans had to be repaid on the first day of filming, which also underlined to the production investors the importance of acknowledging these costs.

6.2.1   OVERVIEW OF THE EUROPEAN SCRIPT FUND TRACK RECORD

The European Script Fund was established in 1988, initially as a pilot programme which ran to December 1990. It was designed as a programme specifically to stimulate the development of film and television projects likely to promote a competitive European film and TV industry. It gives seed money in the form of repayable loans, and is intended to act as a catalyst in raising matching funds for development. This section examines the Fund's pilot phase, its statistical records, its development through to 1994, and the key mechanisms as they were operating in 1995. (SCRIPT's key development schemes are available in Appendix B.)

The history of SCRIPT's supported projects going into production shows a significant increase in its operations during 1994. Between 1989 and 1993, some 55 projects went into production. During 1994 alone, 29 projects went into production (including Team and Incentive Funding projects). This represents an extraordinary percentage rise on the previous 4 years. By November 1984, of the 788 projects receiving development loans, some 125 had either been produced, were in post-production or production, or had start dates. The development/production ratio is beginning to look more healthy, rising from just below 10%, to more than 15% by the end of 1994. By the end of MEDIA I, SCRIPT had awarded 971 project loans, of which 175 had been (or were) in production by the end of 1995.

The application success ratio – shown in the far right percentage column of Table 1 – includes low percentages for Europe's larger territories such as the UK and Italy. This may reflect their domestic difficulties in converting feature projects into production. The national situation was investigated by SCRIPT in the UK and Italy, among others, through the holding of a 'SCRIPT Day'. These sessions were designed to stimulate feed-back on the Fund, including the problems applicants encounter, and further the understanding of SCRIPT's role in the wider development process. The forums were also open to the public (including press) in an effort to raise overall consciousness about development.

Although the UK and Italy appear relatively low in their application success rate, France and Germany are not much higher, despite being the second and fourth highest applicants to the fund. It should also be noted that although Germany appears lower than might be expected, its producers tend to join other funded applicants as co-production or co-financing partners. Hence the lower figure is probably slightly misleading.

In contrast to the relatively low ratios of the larger countries, certain smaller territories have had much larger success ratios. For example, Ireland, Denmark, Portugal, Spain, Greece and the Netherlands have enjoyed

Table 5 Total SCRIPT applications per country (October 1989–November 1994)

Country	Applications received	Applications funded	Percentage
Austria	70	10	14.3
Belgium	267	33	12.4
Denmark	138	32	23.2
Eca	8	2	25.0
Finland	21	5	23.8
France	1063	123	11.6
Germany	704	79	11.2
Greece	269	46	17.1
Hungary	22	4	18.2
Iceland	37	10	27.0
Ireland	392	59	15.1
Italy	851	80	9.4
Luxembourg	10	5	50.0
Netherlands	186	34	18.3
Northern Ireland	5	1	20.0
Norway	18	2	11.1
Others	95	0	0.0
Poland	0	0	0.0
Portugal	116	27	23.3
Spain	405	68	16.8
Sweden	29	2	6.9
Switzerland	94	22	23.4
UK	1857	144	7.7
Totals	6657	788	11.8

success ratios of 15–25%. SCRIPT's staff suggested that these higher figures reflect that producers in these territories are starting to understand what the European Script Fund is, and how to apply in full; to recognize the real value of development support; and to realize that the Fund is not a cultural support system, but an economic tool aimed at helping producers and projects reach the marketplace.

6.2.2 SCRIPT'S EVOLUTION AND EXPERIENCE

Since SCRIPT's operational start in October 1989, certain broad trends have become apparent. The application procedure has changed considerably. According to selection coordinator Christian Routh, 'SCRIPT started off with a pretty basic application form, which we have intentionally made increasingly detailed, so that we can make a more thorough assessment of a project's production and marketing potential'.

No development budget form was included in the original application document. Routh said that this was partly because 'the whole idea of a development budget was new to a lot of countries. It's now a very crucial part of the procedure. It was part of the education process, which involved telling producers, writers and directors what the development process is supposed to be about'.

Two key targets had to be established if the Fund and its applicants were to grow successfully. These were:

1. Explaining clearly what SCRIPT's objectives were and how to apply efficiently.
2. Designing SCRIPT in a way that attracted the best and broadest quality of ideas.

'There was no way to monitor the impact that the loan was having in our early period', recalled Karen Street, responsible for SCRIPT's Second Stage Funding (see Appendix C). 'People were initially assuming that the Fund was for small companies. Our job was to make sure that the loan money was actually being used for development. We are quite broad about what this could include. However, although applicants need to provide evidence of matching finance, we were not that strict in the early period. People tend to defer their fees, but we have toughened this process up considerably', said Street.

According to Renée Goddard, founding secretary general of SCRIPT, the system of deferring fees has been very important. Although not viewed by producers as hard cash, the process of applying to SCRIPT and being made to provide a full development budget has been very instructive. European producers have not tended to account for the high level of time they put into the development process. Too often, the development stage has been accounted for purely in terms of option, treatment and scriptwriting, with the costs of packaging and marketing ignored.

Considering SCRIPT had received some 8800 applications by December 1995 (compared to the 2000 or so feature film projects currently in development and pre-production in Europe), SCRIPT's influence is clearly very significant. The effect of this wider notion of the development process and the potential for changing attitudes cannot be underestimated. However, Street added that is still surprising the number of elements that the applicants either ignore or leave out of their applications, notably on development budget information.

In addition, the team-driven philosophy behind SCRIPT's development strategy had placed a microscope on certain inherent weaknesses in the European industry. Many European producers are still notoriously poor at reading, understanding and being able to criticize treatments and scripts, said key SCRIPT staff. 'There are producers I have met who look at me blankly when I ask about the story itself', explained Routh. Others have reacted with hostility when queried in detail about their financial plans.

Routh also stressed the need to interview the team behind all applications, partly in an effort to encourage the writer/director/producer triangle, but also to assess who is actually driving the project forward. Ironically, a successful SCRIPT application and subsequent loan has, on occasion, triggered a collapse of the project. The reality of dealing with a sum of money either demanded too much commitment or set off multiple disagreements about how to proceed.

SCRIPT's staff also suggested that script analysis reports have had a strong impact on applicants. The process of receiving a third-party report, including detailed feed-back on the script, has encouraged producers to consider another person's views and arguments about the project. 'Sometimes the feed-back is gratefully received, but even when it is rejected, it does force the applicant to formulate arguments to defend the work', said Street. Many producers are careful not to show reader's reports to the writer, but give them a general feel for the suggestions. Rejection and criticism can be taken very badly, and make a project lose valuable momentum.

Overall, there has not been any problem in attracting a high level of applicants. The challenge for the Fund was how to improve applications. As Routh pointed out, 'SCRIPT does not need to attract more applicants; we need to find better projects'. The presentation of applications has greatly improved since 1989. Packages and supporting material, including option rights, cassettes of previous work, treatments and scripts of previous work, legal documentation, letters of support and better efforts to indicate a project's production potential, have been forthcoming. Routh suggested that this improvement has been due to a number of strategies the Fund has introduced. These include: personal interviews with applicants; general discussions on panels and at 'SCRIPT Days', and encouragement to failed applicants to re-apply at a later stage.

6.3 OTHER DEVELOPMENT/TRAINING INITIATIVES

In addition to direct loans toward the development of projects, training and maturing writers' and producers' skills is a critical area of the European film industry. When the MBS feasibility study for the establishment of ACE – Ateliers du Cinéma Européen (the European Film Studio) was carried out in 1991/92, there was widespread agreement that few European producers spend enough time on development.

With the exception of the UK and (arguably) France, the study revealed that there were 'serious concerns about the shortage of high-quality writers in every territory. This stems from the heritage of the *film d'auteur*, in which the director and the writer are usually the same all-powerful individual unwilling to relinquish or share their creative leadership merely for the sake of a wider audience. Until the European producer encourages the development of a substantial stable of writers, it will remain difficult to break the tyranny of the *film d'auteur*'.

The ACE feasibility study went on to stress the need for better quality writing, and the need to keep talented writers interested in continuing to write screenplays and not 'grab the first opportunity to become second-rate directors'.

There lies some of the reasoning behind a range of important producer and writing programmes designed to aid development – including MEDIA Programme's EAVE, and SOURCES, the MBS's involvement in ACE, PILOTS and the Film Business School, and some of the larger screenwriting courses taught in Europe, including France's Equinoxe and the Frank Daniel script workshops. The following analysis examines some of these key initiatives and their progress to date.

6.4   THE MBS APPROACH

Strategically, the MBS played a pro-active role in both the training of talent through an intensive business school approach, and in the pursuit of furthering the specific development process of film and television fiction projects in the market, through its diverse training programmes. In 1993, the MBS consolidated its development strategy by starting up the Television Business School, the Film Business School, PILOTS (the Programme for the International Launch of Television Series) and ACE. The motto applied to the MBS approach was 'Training through Projects'.

6.4.1   ACE – ATELIERS DE CINÉMA EUROPÉEN (THE EUROPEAN FILM STUDIO)

Of specific relevance to feature film development is the ACE Programme, the first permanent development centre for European feature films. ACE is a joint project of the MBS and the Club of European Producers, backed by significant financial support from Le Ville de Paris, Canal Plus, CineVox, PROCIREP, British Screen, Channel 4 and NRW.

Taking media consultant Neil Watson's 1992 feasibility study to its practical conclusion, ACE is built on the belief that 'the creative and financial planning for a project should proceed in tandem', and that the producer is the central nodal point of the project's development. The producer should become the essential bridge between the creative work of the writer and director, and the audience.

Although ACE is a development initiative rather than a training programme, the MBS is hoping that ACE will groom articulate, audience-sensitive film producers who possess an understanding of Europe as both a cultural and a commercial market, fostering a generation of producers who will galvanize Europe's film industry.

ACE kicked off with its first round of producers in November, 1993. Armed with business plans for feature projects, the producers worked to develop their ideas in a way that ACE suggests will 'maximize their chances of reaching the target audience'. According to ACE director Colin Young, ACE decided not to spread its operation over too many producers during its first 6-month period. Out of around 50 applications, ACE took on an initial team of 13 producers.

The 10-day induction seminar at the start of the course provided in-depth analysis and information on the international marketplace for producers. Young believes that although ACE 'probably frustrated producers by making them wait before pitching their own projects, when they come to present them they are very well prepared'. The second workshop (1994) adapted this process by concentrating on individual projects first and dealing with wider issues later.

Above all, ACE producers are encouraged to devise active development strategies for their projects, with a view to moving them into production. Support from an ACE 'godparent' – a senior producer who can help with suggestions and contacts – is a key part of the programme's strategy. However, the 'godparents' do not act as an executive producer. Instead, they advise, support and help with contacts for potential backers, distributors and other professionals who may help the project's development.

In addition, ACE uses a wide selection of top industry professionals as tutors. These consultants help the producer work on specialized elements of their project. For example, script editors and experienced development executives assist with screenplay work; sales executives and distributors assist the producer's efforts to work out the value of the project in the marketplace. The variety of ACE's advice and the ability to test it against a number of experts, rather than simply rely on one supporter, is seen as one of its strategic advantages.

After the first 6-month period, Young explained that the time they will spend with a project will vary depending on its specific status and state of development: 'It is not necessarily setting a period of "x" months, although if a project would be on our books for much more than a year, that would be excessive. ACE does not want to spend 6 months of labour together with a producer, and then say that's it. Projects are often still at a fragile stage, and it would be silly to just abandon them. That's one of the reasons why we cannot spread our operation over too many people'.

Overall, Young believes that the quality of the producers selected is 'first rate'. He stresses that ACE has tried to measure its operation over the initial year and 'improve the transparency of the process so that people realize that we are operating a development company'.

Below, Colin Young explains how the programme operates:

Our specific approach at ACE is to assist in the strategic develop-ment of projects in a more advanced, informed way than the majority of independent European producers work at present.

Having selected our participants, we bring them to Paris in small groups, and we spend a day together. Half a day is spent on the script with experienced editors and evaluators, and half a day on finance.

The finance side concentrates on trying to put a value on the product and working out where the money could come from to reach that target. In a couple of cases it has been clear that the producer expected the value to be much higher than in our financial estimate. And in some cases producers had made certain assumptions in order to get to their valuations. Figures would need to be revised downwards if those assumptions about the script or elements of the package were not subsequently met.

When ACE talks about placing a 'value' on a project, what we are doing is examining the elements of the script, the likely cost of its production, the director, the principal cast and the language of production. In two or three cases, we have a 'Plan A' and a 'Plan B'. For example, we keep the same story, but package an unknown director and cast. The production cost may have to be lower, or elements be changed. Or, in other cases, a project will move upwards – a higher profile star or director – and the budget will go up if we think it can break out into the international market.

Our overall attitude about production finance is that we would rather expose ACE projects to risk investment than just get finance from subsidies and TV licenses. Our projects are encouraged to meet the market. It opens the whole process up. Of course they need to be concerned about not losing control, especially if the project has a very high commercial upside. But I believe that we can encourage some courageous decisions and help support the European producer.

6.5　SOURCES (STIMULATING OUTSTANDING RESOURCES FOR CREATIVE EUROPEAN SCREENWRITING)

SOURCES was the result of a proposal for an initiative in the craft of screenwriting, which was adopted on June 25, 1992, by the MEDIA Programme Committee. The background to SOURCES goes back to the Council's decision of December 21, 1990, to announce a specific action in the field of 'script doctoring'. The Council acknowledged that following consultations with European experts, an enhancement of the craft of European screenwriting was possible by setting up an autonomous project for the coordination and development of training for screenwriters. SCRIPT's experience had pointed to the need for more specific training in the craft of screenwriting.

The main action of SOURCES was to hold script development workshops for a maximum of six professional screenwriters per tutor. Producers were encouraged to visit the workshop if they are involved in a project. Each workshop consists of two 7-day sessions. In between these, there is a re-writing period of approximately 12 weeks. Contact and training is carried out by script experts, with whom writers can keep in touch with during the intermediate period.

SOURCES was clearly starting to play a role in screenwriting training, although it has taken some time to find its feet. According to SOURCES' former director Dick Willemsen, 'The writers it is starting to benefit are those who have left film school, but who are not yet really ready for the market'. His comments about the programme's approach are as follows:

> Our training is not about telling people what or how to write, but encouraging them to find their own voice. We are project-led, not theory-led. More than 90% of script development is about making a writer realize that they are writing for an audience. We have to tell our participants this time and time again. We hear phrases such as: "I'm writing this for film, not TV, so I can do what I like ..." Our job is to convince them otherwise. We also help writers on how to present their work, an element that many of them have no real idea about.

The advice provided by SOURCES includes: explaining how many minutes per page are established; writing and presenting synopsis outlines; how to make your story stand out of a pile of 300; general aesthetic presentation; and additional directions, good pacing and rhythm, and readability.

6.6 THE FRANK DANIEL SCRIPT WORKSHOPS

Frank Daniel and his team of script 'doctors' have been re-activated in Europe since 1991, thanks to support from the NRW, SOURCES, SCALE and the European Script Fund, among other partners. Up until 1992 three workshops had benefitted 75 writers and editors in Europe, and a further eight workshops were held during 1993/94. Each session hosts approximately 24 European writers with scripts, treatments or ideas.

A former scriptwriter of some 19 films and director of four features, Czech-born Frank Daniel has held top film teaching posts in Prague, New York and Los Angeles before helping Robert Redford to set up the Sundance Institute in Utah, in 1981. Hence he brings both an American and European perspective to the industry. In the early 1980s Daniel came back to Europe to teach script workshops, where he helped film-makers, including Jaco van Dormael (*Toto the Hero*), Dominique Deruddere (*Crazy Love*) and Marion Hansel (*Dust*).

The workshop emphasizes the importance of group discussions. Producers attached to the projects are encouraged to attend the treatment and script sessions. Mornings are dedicated to intensive sessions with the writer's tutors. Alternately, afternoons are dedicated to the screening and following analysis of exemplary films.

Sources spoken to for this book were generally positive about the courses. 'You can learn a lot from his sessions, partly because they are clear, simple to understand. Seeing a film twice is useful, because on many courses these film analyses are useless when examining a film most people are seeing for the first time recently', said one commentator. However, others pointed out that the group workshops are not as 'vibrant' as they could be: 'People are supposed to criticize, but the individuals tend not to, mainly to avoid being criticized back', said one commentator. However, in general, the feeling from the MBS research suggested that this is a worthwhile contribution towards the development of European talent.

6.7 EQUINOXE

Probably the most significant development initiative in France other than the CNC's 'Aide Au Developpément' scheme is Equinoxe. This special scriptwriting workshop was held for the first time in Bordeaux, France, in September 1993. Operating in association with the Sundance Institute, Equinoxe follows a similar line of teaching to the Frank Daniel's approach.

Launched at the initiative of Nöelle Deschamps, head of ID, one of the very few independent development houses in France, Equinoxe provided seven senior tutors – including Andrew Birkin, Larry Konner, Patrick Dewolf and Shawn Slovo – to help seven screenwriters work on specific scripts.

Equinoxe, heavily supported by the CNC and Canal Plus, along with British Screen and the European Script Fund, became a twice yearly event and held its second session at the end of March. The CNC, Canal Plus, British Screen and SCRIPT each nominates two students, with the Sundance Institute sending a further one.

Sony Pictures Entertainment has entered into a 3-year sponsorship of the programme as from October, 1994. In return, Sony has a First Look arrangement on the projects developed with the support of the programme. However, this does not lead to automatic financing of the films which result from this relationship. Sony also has the right to send one participant to each session.

Noëlle Deschamps, founder of the Equinoxe programme, explains below how the programme operates:

> Equinoxe is designed to place a higher value on the script and the screenwriter. We want to make it understood that a script is the backbone for everything else that follows. We want to make the authors more demanding and to learn the best habits. But we do

not attempt to teach a precise methodology, like how to write a good beginning scene, or a good end.

Practically, Equinoxe has a project selection process which starts in July of each year for the October session. Each of the supporting bodies behind Equinoxe, including the CNC, British Screen, SCRIPT, Sundance and Canal Plus Ecriture, send five or six scripts that they have pre-selected. I then select personally two from each, although I am in the process of setting up a selection committee to work with me. At the same time, I decide the tutors who I feel will best fit with the eight or nine scripts selected, in the hope that they will be able to bring something different to the projects and provide an international perspective. This means working with real professionals and exposing the scripts to different national approaches.

I hope to include a wider range of countries as Equinoxe evolves. Equinoxe is happy to take on strong commercial projects, because by making more films work in the marketplace, the concept of development will spread. Producers will be forced to pay more for scripts and, in turn, will demand more from them.

6.8   FIRST FILM FOUNDATION

The UK-based First Film Foundation (FFF), which enjoys charitable trust status, is an important development operation for young and first-time film-makers. The FFF was set up in 1989 and is financed by industry sponsorship. It runs out of London and has around 30 projects in development at any one time.

According to FFF's director Ivan McTaggart, the Foundation acts as 'a development house for new film-makers by providing training, guidance and facilities for the development of their projects'. What it does not offer is straight development finance for specific projects.

The FFF handles scripts, treatments and a range of enquiries about first-time issues and strategies. Feedback on all material is forthcoming, and more advanced workshops are held for young writers, directors, producers and actors. It has an excellent track-record at introducing promising talent to more experienced professionals and helping debut projects reach production. The Foundation also has access to legal, accounting and administrative services.

The strategic element that the FFF highlights is that development initiatives are not just about raising or accessing money. They can also play a critical role in the training and building of new careers. For young or first-time film-makers, there is often a significant gap between getting a grip on the industry and then managing to access much of the above support outlined in this chapter. The FFF serves to close that gap.

EDITOR'S NOTE

MEDIA II, the new EU audiovisual programme, was not underway as this book went to press. One development 'Intermediary Organisation' and one training IO will replace SCRIPT, SOURCES and the MEDIA BUSINESS SCHOOL's current status. For further information please speak to your local MEDIA Desk.

What next? 7

Feature film development is clearly in a state of transition when examined within the overall state of the European film industry. From being generally under-valued and misconceived a decade ago, Europe's film industry is starting to place more emphasis on the importance of the development process. However, the levels of emphasis vary considerably from territory to territory.

While development's profile has clearly risen, it is apparent that there are no uniform rules or consistently applied practices that fit the European industry in the way, for example, they do in Hollywood. This may not necessarily be a disadvantage, given that a flexible, creative approach can provide very beneficial results. But where 'flexible' just means a one-draft script being pushed in front of the cameras it is simply destructive to the growth and development of an overall industry. Without setting down hard-and-fast conclusions, the following key points that have been raised in this publication are summarized as follows.

7.1 A CHANGING PERCEPTION

Feature film producers across Europe are more actively involved in and aware of the role of development of projects than they were 5 years ago, and considerably more than a decade ago. In general, the level of awareness about development in Europe has improved, but it remains very inconsistent.

For example, southern countries such as Italy, Spain and Greece, have a very different concept of what development means when compared to northern territories, and most notably the UK. However, certain aspects of the southern states' approaches have started to show positive changes. For example, recent development training for scriptwriters and producers in Greece is a remarkable step forward.

7.2　NO STUDIO UMBRELLAS

Europe has no studios that operate on the same scale as Hollywood. Few major companies are committed to feature film production at a significant level. Consequently, without proper capitalization, an independent company investing in feature films survives mainly from earning money when in production. Development remains a high-risk, expensive area of a producer's overhead.

However, during the time this book was in preparation, a number of changes seem to have taken place. For example, a number of larger, cash-rich companies have significantly increased their commitment to film production. PolyGram Filmed Entertainment has now grown into a mini-major studio, albeit operating through subsidiary film companies rather than under one studio lot. Chrysalis Films has been established, supporting the development of a number of producers but with mixed results to date. Chargeurs has increased its development executive division in a specific move to hunt down new projects to develop and produce. Although still to take the full plunge into production, Bertelsmann is now close to putting into action a fully-fledged film operation.

Five years from now, the above companies – and a handful of others – will clearly play an even greater role in financing feature film development than they do already. The financial support and ability to develop larger amounts of projects is clearly a good aspect of this trend.

7.3　THE FRAGMENTATION PROBLEM

The experience of the European Script Fund and other public funds has demonstrated the problems of giving loans to single writers for development of their projects. The lack of completed films from such loans has proved how hard it is for a writer to find producers and production finance, and get their scripts made. Writers in Europe need a better framework within which to work, and stronger links with producers.

Sigrid Narjes, managing director of International Management Consulting, one of the only agencies that represents writers, directors and actors on the continent, has argued that writers need more support: 'An institution should be established across Europe that is similar to the Writer's Guild of America (WGA). There is not enough protection for writers, and no overall institution exists where writers and producers can register their material. This would probably enhance trust between writer and producers. Europe's film and television industry would also benefit professionally if more talent agencies that represent writers and directors, as well as actors, were created'.

While the truly big companies appear to be increasing their commitment towards development, the problem is the fragmented nature of the smaller

European producers. The levels spent on development within the majority of medium and smaller companies has depended heavily on available funds; principally past profits and ownership of rights which can be mortgaged, or direct development subsidies. These elements remain relatively precarious and inconsistent.

For a medium to smaller company, the cost and risk of developing material is a real business burden. The level of work required to convert a developing project into production is very high. Slates of 30 films mean that only five or six are really on the 'front burner' for conversion at any one time. In other words, only around 25% of a company's slate is actually undergoing fully-fledged development at any one time. Professionals interviewed throughout the book have emphasized that what matters is the 'quality' of the development strategy, rather than the 'quantity' of projects on a slate.

7.4 CRITICISMS BEING ANSWERED

Many professionals continue to argue forcefully that not enough time is being given to the development and preparation of films in Europe. Screenplays are still being rushed into production without enough attention, professional script editing and drafts. However, the level of criticism aimed at the above failing has been strongly voiced over the last 2 years, and some effect seems to have taken place as a result. Many producers felt that the public funding systems (especially in Germany) were starting to take note of the above criticisms. For example, the new policies adopted by the Filmboard Berlin-Brandenburg, including higher sums towards development budgets, were cited as an encouraging example.

Such changes of tactics are important because they influence the way producers approach and consider the development process. For example, many producers still do not know how to construct a development budget. Too often the development stage has been accounted for purely in terms of option, treatment and scriptwriting, with the costs of packaging and marketing ignored. Again, the European Script Fund, along with the MBS's 'training through projects' approach, started to help combat this problem to a certain extent.

7.5 MORE DEVELOPMENT FINANCE AVAILABLE

The overall level of funds available in the public sector for feature film development have risen significantly over the last 5 years. Specifically, the level of national public spending on development has risen by approximately ECU 12m since 1991. This rise has partly been due to the European Script Fund's operations, which have been closely monitored by national funding bodies.

While public support has gradually experienced a positive sea-change toward development over the last decade, it has not been beyond criticism. The overall level of monitoring by both public and private funds is still low and unsophisticated. If development is to become an industrial tool, in the same way for example that 'Research & Development' is applied to scientific or manufacturing industries, then better record-keeping and monitoring will be required. Any new development mechanisms operating under MEDIA 2 would do well to take such observations on board.

It is also notable that SCRIPT's Incentive Funding scheme for companies has been taken up – in adapted forms – by France's 'Aide Au Développement' scheme (CNC) and by the NRW, and is under consideration by other public funds. Concentrating more public development support in larger companies has been seen as a strategic way of strengthening the industry.

7.6 INVESTING IN LARGER COMPANIES

The argument for investing more heavily in bigger companies as an incentive mechanism was put forward by PolyGram's Michael Kuhn. 'The European film industry is not weak because of lack of production. It is weak because it lacks strong, financially stable entertainment companies that are able to produce a slate of films that are competitive with US product and then market those films around the world. If the European Union wants to achieve its vision of an economically viable European audiovisual sector, it has to encourage the development of viable entertainment companies'.

Kuhn goes on to argue that the EU should encourage companies seeking funding for a slate of European-based films as opposed to single picture finance. 'This will allow investors to spread their risk over a larger number of films and facilitate the production of a large catalogue of European films'. A system of long-term guarantees, low interest loans and off-balance sheet funding are some of the ideas Kuhn's case puts forward.

Joint ventures between different international partners are starting to have an effect on the level and, more importantly, the quality of development executed. The recent growth of trans-Atlantic First Look and House-keeping deals are helping to cement relationships between the development/production area and the distributor/end-user. They also help to combat the current heavy fragmentation that European producers suffer.

On the other hand, there are increasingly fewer sources of both development and production finance, while that finance is becoming controlled by fewer, larger entities. Some see a potential danger in concentrating resources on the bigger companies and, by definition, the larger film projects. They argue that this is not necessarily playing to Europe's cultural and commercial strengths.

However, development is a pragmatic combination of creative and financial demands. Senior producers suggest that if a company can find a strong partner with whom to develop a script or a slate of projects, who also has the capacity to subsequently finance the production, then it is better off going with that system. It is also possible to point to PolyGram Filmed Entertainment, for example, and the company's ability to support low-budget, culturally specific feature films through its production 'label' approach toward development and production.

7.7 THE BROADCASTER CATCH

Professionals stressed that feature film development has been heavily influenced by European broadcasters, specifically by the commissioning editor model. This model usually takes the following pattern: the idea is normally the writer's, who is then left alone to write a draft. Minor modifications are then made before the project is shot for TV. 'That process has nothing to do with the process adopted by commercial film companies, which is much more akin to product development', argued David Puttnam.

However, certain broadcasters have taken a pro-active approach to film development. Notable examples include UK's Channel 4 and France's Canal Plus, who have respectively set aside considerable finance for development activity and, in the case of Canal Plus Ecriture, set up training and development schemes for writers and producers.

7.8 TRAINING BEYOND 2000

New public funding mechanisms have clearly had an impact on the state of development. However, the underlying importance of training should be incorporated in future strategies. Professional training should be widespread, and focussed on both first-time talent and maturing film-makers. It should be aimed at producers, writers, directors, administrators, company executives and any other relevant professionals, so that the importance of the development process becomes automatically incorporated into new planning and business strategies.

7.9 TAKING RISKS FOR THE FUTURE

Within the overall perspective of the European film industry's future, development could, and should, play a vital role. However, if that role is to be fulfilled, many of the criticisms, observations and positive new practices explored in this book will need to be implemented and taken further. There is a tendency for European film practitioners to pay lip-service to research and documentation, rather than taking it to heart and acting vigorously on its findings. The raised profile, professional practice and continued emphasis on development cannot be overstated. If Europe, both as a Union and as a network of interconnected territories, can place development up at the front of its audiovisual industry's agenda, the European film industry will be a significantly stronger place 10 years from now.

Appendix A: National public sources of development finance – country by country

8.1 AUSTRIA

Austrian Film Fund
Spittelberggasse 3, A-1070 Vienna, Austria
Tel: +43 1 52697 30406; Fax: +43 1 52697 30440
Enquiries: Mr Hruza

Activities and details:

* The AFF is the main source of public funding in Austria.
* From its annual federal budget of ECU 725 000 it supports: script development, treatment and acquisition of rights.
* Awards are around ECU 7250 each.
* Varying amounts are also awarded for project development.
* Larger awards for project development beyond just script writing are available. Amounts vary.

8.2 BELGIUM

Ministère de la Culture et de la Communication: Direction de l'audiovisuel
(Ministry of Culture, French Community: Audiovisual Section)
44, Boulevard Leopold II, 1080 Brussels, Belgium
Tel: +32 2 413 2311; Fax: +32 2 413 2068
Enquiries: Henri Ingberg/Serge Maurant

Activities and details:

* The total budget is ECU 3.5m.

- About ECU 500 000 is available for development support of features, shorts and documentaries.
- Both domestic producers and writers can apply.
- The fund is strictly for French language projects.
- Loans for feature scripts is ECU 6–8000.
- The concept of 'matching fund' is applied (the producer has to share 50% of the development budget).
- Producers are required to start repaying loans as soon as they receive any returns from the film's proceeds.

Ministerie van de Vlaamse Gemeenschap (Ministry of Flemish Culture)
Kolonienstraat 31, 1000 Brussels, Belgium
Tel: +32 2 510 35 66; Fax: +32 2 510 3651
Enquiries: Derek Coolos/W. Juwet

Activities and details:

- The Fund has been in operation since January 1994.
- Script awards available to writers only.
- Pre-production awards available to producers.
- All awards for projects in the Flemish language.
- Scriptwriters are awarded ECU 7500 per script.
- Pre-production support is between ECU 37 500 to 125 000.
- Applications must be sent on forms provided (16 copies needed).
- Flemish audiovisual selection committee decides on awards.
- Deadlines are the last day of every month.

8.3   CENTRAL AND EASTERN EUROPE

8.3.1   BULGARIA

Bulgaria Film Fund
c/o National Film Centre, 2, Dondukov Bul., Sofia 1000, Bulgaria
Tel: +359 2 883 8317; Fax: +369 2 873 626
Enquiries: Dimiter Dereliev (President)

Activities and details:

- Founded in 1991.
- Only public source of development finance.
- Awards money on a script by script basis.
- Awards for development are at around ECU 1300.
- Ten scripts were developed in 1993.

8.3.2   CIS AND THE BALTIC STATES

Committee of Cinematography of the Russian Federation (Roskomkino)
7 Mal. Gnezdnikovsk Lane, 103877 Moscow, Russia

Tel: +7 122 229 7005 or 229 8224
Enquiries: Armen Medvedev (Chairman)/Valery N. Rjabinsky (Deputy Chairman)

Activities and details:

* All details have to be requested from the above address.

Eisenstein-Gemini Foundation
c/o Gemini Film International, Post Box 192, 101000 Moscow, Russia
Tel: +7 95 921 0597 or 921 1795; Fax: +7 95 921 2394

Activities and details:

* Founded in 1991.
* Script awards given on an annual basis.
* All awards sponsored by Gemini Film, which distributes Warner Bros and Columbia TriStar films in Russia.
* 1993's award was around 50 million rubles, but the prestige is more useful than the cash value.

8.3.3   CZECH REPUBLIC

The State Fund of the Czech Republic for the Development and Support of Cinematography
Valdstcjnske nam. 4, 118 11 Prague 1, Czech Republic
Tel: +422 513 1111; Fax: +422 451 0897 or 537 055
Enquiries: Andrej Stankovic (Chairman)

Activities and details:

* Development details from above address.
* Nine projects were supported in 1993.
* Nineteen projects were supported for production in 1994.
* Budget for 1995 is around ECU 1m.

Milos Havel Foundation
Krizeneckeho nam., 322, 150 00 Prague 5, Czech Republic
Tel: +422 6707 1111; Fax: +422 2451 0628
Enquiries: Yvona Dobranska

Activities and details:

* Founded in the beginning of 1993.
* Supported by McDonalds, which has leased a Barrandov property.
* Open to anyone with permanent residence in the Czech Republic.
* Submissions close at the end of March and the end of September each year.

* Amounts awarded: 10 000–60 000 Czech crowns.

8.3.4 HUNGARY

Hungarian Motion Picture Foundation
Szalai u 10, 1054 Budapest, Hungary
Tel: +36 1 112 6417; Fax: +36 1 268 0070
Enquiries: Lorant Szanto (Secretary)/Ferenc Kohalmi (General Secretary)

Activities and details:

* Projects selected on a script by script basis all year round.
* Details need to be sought from the above address.

8.3.5 POLAND

The Polish Script Agency
Chelmska 21, 00724 Warsaw, Poland
Tel: +48 22 411211 (extn 265); Fax: +48 22 415891
Enquiries: Gicek Kondracki (Deputy Director)/Pawel Luczwnski

Activities and details:

* Modelled after the French CNC approach.
* Loans are made for development and have to be repaid if the film goes into production.
* Scripts are accepted by a committee.

Film Production Agency
Film Packages Department, Pulawska Str. 61, Room Nr. 108, Warsaw, Poland
Tel: +48 22 455316 or 454041; Fax: +48 22 455586
Enquiries: Buguslaw Scwajkowska

Activities and details:

* All application enquiries have to be made personally to the above address.

8.3.6 ROMANIA

Romanian National Film Centre
25, Thomas Masaryk Str., Sector 2, Bucharest, Romania
Tel: +40 611 2515; Fax: +40 211 3688
Enquiries: Alexandru Marin (Vice President)

Activities and details:

- Founded in 1990.
- Only source of public development finance in the country.
- Support for scripts are selected by a funding board on a project by project basis.
- All application details, including amount of the loan, from the above address.

8.3.7 SLOVAK REPUBLIC

State Fund of the Culture ProSlovakia
Dobrovicova 12, 813 31 Bratislava, Slovak Republic
Tel: +42 7 456 495; Fax: +42 7 456 494
Enquiries: Eduard Grecner

Activities and details:

- Virtually no film activity in the country at present.
- 1993 saw six projects supported with production grants of around ECU 600 000.
- No details on development finance available/enquire at above address.

8.3.8 OTHER FUNDS

Aid to Co-Productions with Countries of Central and Oriental Europe (CNC)
11, Rue Galilee, 75116 Paris, France
Tel: +33 1 44 34 38 04; Fax: +33 1 44 34 38 40
Enquiries: Cecile Jodlowski

Activities and details:

- Central and Eastern European producers may apply for development support.
- A French co-producer is essential for application.
- Strong cultural ideas accepted.
- The majority of the budget goes to production.
- Since 1990, 71 films have been backed, with 39 completed and 20 distributed in Europe.
- Development support varies, but projects can be submitted without being fully developed; if the fund backs it, a commitment of support is given, helping additional finance to be raised.
- Money has to be repaid if the film goes into profit.

Films developed and produced with the Fund's support:
Urga
Riaba, My Chicken

Hartley-Merrill Prize
Country contacts for the Hartley-Merrill Prize:

Poland
Jacek Kondraki (Head of the Polish Script Agency)
The Polish Script Agency, Chelmska 21, 00 724 Warsaw, Poland
Tel: +48 22 411211 (extn 265); Fax: +48 22 415891

Hungary
Levi Malnay
HBO, Hungarian division.
Fax: +36 1 181 2377

Russia and the CIS
Tanya Nazarova
First Talent Russian Agency
Fax: +7 0952 302 938

Georgia
Piotr Khotianovski
Local representative
Fax: +7 8832 294 662

Activities and details:

- The Hartley-Merrill Prize is an important award for scriptwriters which was founded in 1989 by RKO pictures chairman Ted Hartley and his wife Dina Merrill; it is not a fund.
- Coordinators in each country choose the best script submitted and send them to an international jury of distinguished writers, actors and directors.
- The recipient receives a cash award and travel and accommodation expenses at the Sundance Film Institute's scriptwriters' workshop.
- Local runners-up benefit because selection by the local board often results in development support being released from other national film funds based on the distinction of being selected.

8.4   DENMARK

The Danish Film Institute
   Store Sondervoldstroede 4, 1419 Copenhagen, Denmark

Tel: +45 31 57 6500; Fax: +45 31 57 6700
Enquiries: Mona Jensen (Acting Director)

Activities and details:

- Subsidies for script writing of Danish feature films.
- Subsidies for the development and pre-production of Danish feature films.
- Writers, producers and directors are eligible for development support; maximum payment is 90% of the rights.
- Treatment support for writers of around ECU 1300.
- Full screenplay support of ECU 4000 for re-writing and editing, but not exceeding ECU 20 000 in total.
- Pre-production subsidy of 90% maximum of budgeted costs.
- Manuscript research support, with maximum of ECU 5200.
- Recommendations are submitted to the Board by a group of three film consultants working independently of each other; these are appointed initially for 3 years and cannot exceed 6 years at the Institute.
- First payment can be made to the writer; subsequent payments must be made to attached producer.
- Acquisition of rights for property intended to be made into the project.

8.5   FINLAND

Finnish Film Foundation
Kanavakatu 12, 00160 Helsinki, Finland
Tel: +3580 6220 300; Fax: +3580 6220 3050

Activities and details:

- Awards for script development, planning and pre-production.
- Support in any form is only granted to a Finnish holder of the rights.
- Script support is granted primarily to an applicant who can present written proof of a producer's interest in the project.
- All option rights of adapted material must be proved.
- Applications must be accompanied by a synopsis and project description.

Films developed by the Finnish Film Foundation:
Seasick
Going to Kansas City
The Minister of State

8.6 FRANCE

Avances Sur Recettes
Centre National de la Cinématographie (CNC), 12 rue Lubeck, 75116 Paris, France
Tel: +33 1 44 34 34 40; Fax: +33 1 47 55 04 91
Enquiries: André Avignon

Activities and details:

(1) Interest-free loans for film projects about to go into pre-production:

* A maximum of two installments of up to ECU 76 000.
* Producer must submit agreement showing copyright, project's budget and the financial plan.
* The applicant must have produced a film previously which received public-sector aid.
* The producer must start principal photography within 24 months from being notified of the loan.
* Re-submissions are allowed by projects rejected after changes have been made.

(2) Aid for script re-writing:

* Some ECU 300 000–450 000 per year is spent directly on 're-writes'.
* Single writers are awarded advances of around ECU 8000.
* Team-written and developed script awards go up to ECU 20 000.
* A further ECU 60 000–80 000 is available for sending scriptwriters to workshops.

Aide Au Développement
Centre National de la Cinématographie (CNC), 12 rue Lubeck, 75116 Paris, France
Tel: +33 1 44 34 34 40; Fax: +33 1 47 55 04 91
Enquiries: c/o André Avignon

Activities and details:

* The previous version of AAD pre-1994 had ECU 1.52m budget a year.
* The new AAD spent as much as ECU 3.05 million in 1995.
* Single projects and companies with multiple projects can apply.
* The first round in April 1994 spent ECU 1.2m and 27 awards were given.
* Nine of the awards were for single projects.
* The value of the awards ranged from ECU 18 000 to 165 000.
* Loans are repayable on the first day of production.
* AAD money can only be spent on the script elements of a film's

development, including: research of subject matter, the purchase and optioning of rights, writing, re-writing, and translation and documentation.
- Pre-production costs are not covered.
- The money is paid directly to producers, and not to directors or writers.
- Applications from above address.

Maison des Ecrivains
Centre National de la Cinématographie (CNC), 12 rue Lubeck, 75116 Paris, France
Tel: +33 1 44 34 34 40; Fax: +33 1 47 55 04 91
Enquiries: André Avignon

Activities and details:

- Aid for first treatment of scripts is ECU 3500.
- Aid for subsequent script development is ECU 10 000.
- Subsequent aid is only granted on a selective basis and for projects which received aid for the first treatment.
- Projects submitted should be no more than a 12-page synopsis.
- The author must not have written more than two scripts in the previous 4 years.
- The writer(s) must be working under contract for a producer.
- The producer must have made at least one film meeting CNC requirements or hold a professional CNC certificate.
- The writer(s) must be paid a minimum of ECU 20 000.

PROCIREP
20 bis rue La Boetie, 75008 Paris, France
Tel: +33 1 40 07 10 27; Fax: +33 1 40 07 07 65
Enquiries: Mme Seror

Activities and details:

- Aide Aux Développement des Longs Métrages.
- An award to be paid to the producer, not to the writer or director.
- The bursary, which is not expected to be repaid, can only be spent on writers, adaptations and rights.
- PROCIREP may grant aid on the condition that the company must be financing at least 50% of the development expenses itself.
- It is an award of somewhere between ECU 18 200 and 76 000.
- Applicants must be experienced, with at least one feature film or 10 short films already produced.
- In 1993, PROCIREP funded 60 re-writes.
- Between 60 and 70% of the applications considered are approved.

8.7   GERMANY

8.7.1   GERMAN FEDERAL DEVELOPMENT SUPPORT

Filmförderungsanstalt (German Federal Film Board)
Bundesanstalt des Öffentlichen Rechts, Postfach 30 18 08, Berlin; and
Budapester Straße 41, 10787 Berlin, Germany
Tel: +49 30 254 0900; Fax: +49 30 262 8976

Activities and details:

- Script development subsidies available.
- Applicants must be scriptwriters backed by a producer.
- A project description and a treatment of one of the scenes is required.
- Generally up to ECU 15 500 per projects, but can be as much as ECU 40 000 in exceptional cases.
- Scripts that have received other types of public-sector support are excluded.
- Payments are made in two equal installments: 50% when the aid is approved and the rest upon examination and approval of the script.

Bundesministerium des Innerns (BMI) (Federal Ministry of the Interior)
BMI-Filmreferat, Postfach 170290, 53108 Bonn, Germany
Tel: +49 228 681 5569; Fax: +49 228 681 4665
Enquiries: Detlef Flotho

Activities and details:

- Script development subsidies available.
- Applicant must be the scriptwriter.
- The total annual budget is around ECU 40 000.
- Sums are up to ECU 8000 in most individual script cases, but subsidies of up to ECU 25 000 have been awarded in exceptional circumstances.
- The Ministry also provides editing and counselling services on request to supported scriptwriters.
- Five screenplay drafts were supported in 1994.

8.7.2   GERMAN REGIONAL DEVELOPMENT SUPPORT

Filmstiftung Nordrhein-Westfalen GmbH
Kaistrasse 14, 40221 Düsseldorf, Germany
Tel: +49 211 930 500; Fax: +49 211 930 505
Enquiries: Manuela Stehr

Activities and details:

(1) Loans for script development

- Producers, writers and directors can apply.
- Producers must already be working with a screenwriter at the time of the application.
- At least one of the partners must be based in Nordrhein-Westfalen.
- If the applicant is a producer, they must undertake to make the resulting film in the region, as far as possible.
- If the applicant is a scriptwriter, they must undertake to offer the script to a producer resident in Nordrhein-Westfalen.
- Development funding is available for theatrical and TV films.
- Treatment and development of a dialogue scene must be included in the application.
- Funding is granted as a conditionally repayable, interest-free loan.
- Payments are made in three equal installments: on signature of the agreement; on delivery of a first draft; and on approval of the final script by the selection committee.
- Twelve scripts were supported in 1994, with a total investment of ECU 240 000.

(2) Loans for production preparation

- Interest-free, repayable loans.
- Producers and directors can apply.
- At least one of the applicants has to be resident in Nordrhein-Westfalen and the film must be produced in the region.
- Amounts vary depending on the project, although most single projects are eligible for up to ECU 100 000.
- A treatment of the script must be enclosed for application.
- The loan can be up to 80% of the overall development budget.
- Repayment conditions: within 6 months of the start of principal photography, or on pre-sale of the rights to a third party, in which case the loan becomes immediately due and repayable.
- If the film has not been produced within 36 months from payment of the final instalment of the loan, the film's rights pass to the Fund; however, the scriptwriter may apply for reversion of the script's copyright.
- If the script is also subsidized by WDR, they acquire the screening rights.
- A total of nine projects were supported for production in 1994 with an investment of ECU 490 000.

Filmboard Berlin-Brandenburg GmbH
Postfach 900 402, 14440 Potsdam-Babelsberg, Germany

Tel: +49 331 721 2859; Fax: +49 331 721 2848
Enquiries: Klaus Keil (Director)

Activities and details:

- Operating since September 1994.
- Only producers can apply for development support.
- In addition to development, loans are also available for packaging, marketing and pre-production costs.
- Total development and pre-production budget of ECU 2–2.5m
- The fund is deliberately flexible about the limits of the amounts loaned.
- Conditionally repayable loans can be granted for up to 70% of the development budget of the project presented.
- Development loans have to be repaid on first day of principal photography and also if any of the project's licensing rights are sold to a third party before principal photography commences.
- In the first round of development support, 11 applications were received; decisions were made on 10 projects, and funding was granted to two projects amounting to approximately ECU 115 000.
- In the first round of packaging and pre-production support, 11 applications were received; six were decided upon, and four features and one documentary received a total of ECU 310 000.

Films supported by Filmboard Berlin-Brandenburg:

Private Service
Rififi in New York
Out of Darkness
Sin

Filmförderungs GmbH
Friedensallee 14-16,
22765 Hamburg, Germany
Tel: +49 40 398 370; Fax: +49 40 398 3710
Enquiries: Alfred Hürmer, Eva Hubert

Activities and details:

- Script funding – maximum DM 100 000 paid out.
- Only producers and writers may apply.
- Connection with Hamburg essential.
- Treatment, scene of dialogue required.
- Bio-filmography and budget required.
- Project development – up to 80% of costs, maximum DM 200 000.
- Only producers can apply, and provide 20% of own funds.
- Support funds are generally provided as conditionally repayable loans.

Film FernsehFonds Bayern
c/o Bayerisches Filmzentrum Geiselgasteig
Bavariafilmplatz 7
82031 Geiselgasteig, Germany
Tel: +49 89 649 81; Fax: +49 89 649 81
For financial transactions call:
Tel: +49 89 212 42429; Fax: +49 89 212 42509
Enquiries: Dr Herbert Huber, Dr Klaus Schaefer

Activities and details:

* Total budget of DM 45m.
* Part of the Bavarian State Government's media promotion programme.
* Partly repayable subsidies for writing and development of film scripts with a limit to be announced by mid-1996.
* Applicant must be the author of the script and reside in Germany.

LTS-Wirtschaft (Lower Saxony)
Hamburger Allee 4, 30161 Hanover, Germany
Tel: +49 511 361 57 80; Fax: +49 511 361 57 06
Enquiries: Mr Engelking

Activities and details:

* Non-repayable subsidies of up to ECU 1250 for writers.
* Up to ECU 15 000 for full script development.
* Applicant must be the author of the script.
* Applications must include a draft script.
* The script development applicant must apply with a producer resident in Lower Saxony.

Schleswig-Holstein
Kulturelle Filmförderung Schleswig-Holstein e.V., Filmbüro
Königstraße 21, 23552 Lübeck
Tel: +49 451 716 49; Fax: +49 451 75 374
Enquiries: Jan Hammerich, Angela Buske

Activities and details:

* Overall budget: DM 450 000

(1) Project development:

* Maximum of DM 15 000 can be granted.
* Awarded as grants to filmmakers from Schleswig-Holstein, and others with a local connection.
* Scripts: no funding of scripts for feature-length films.

Medien- und Filmgesellschaft Baden-Württemberg mbH (MFG)
Film Aid Department

Friedrichstraße 24 (L-Bank)
D-70174 Stuttgart
Tel: +49 711 122 2833; Fax: +49 711 122 2834
Enquiries: Gabriele Röthemayer

Activities and details:

- Founded in October 1995. Has an annual global budget of DM 10m; the fund's shareholders are the Land of Baden-Württemberg, and the two local public broadcasters SDR and SWF.
- The fund's general requirements: (1) the project's cultural quality and (2) an economic interest in the project relating to Baden-Württemberg or (3) some other reference to B-W.
- Aid can be offered in the form of a conditional interest-free loan for the preparation work necessary for a production, particularly for the writing of screenplays. Each payment should not exceed DM 50 000.
- Those entitled to apply are screenplay writers, producers and directors.
- The application for screenwriting support should be accompanied by a treatment or exposé with a scene of dialogue. The film's plot, structure, and dramatical development must be evident in the exposé.
- Must be submitted with seven copies.
- Repayment is due should the rights to the assisted works be alienated six months after shooting has started.
- If the project also receives production support from the fund, an agreement could be reached whereby, instead of a repayment being made, the preparation funding becomes part of the production support.
- Should, three years following the handover of the grant, the project not have been realised, then the rights attached through the use of this grant are handed over to the MFG.
- On repaying the share of the aid grant allotted to the work of the author, the grant recipient is entitled to demand a retransfer of the rights to the screenplay.

MSH, Gesellschaft zur Förderung audiovisueller Werke in Schleswig-Holstein mbH
Königstraße 21, 23552 Lübeck
Tel: +49 451 122 4109; Fax: +49 451 719 78
Enquiries: Andrea Künsemüller

Activities and details:

- Overall budget: DM 1m a year.

(1) Project preparation:

- Maximum grants awarded are DM 100 000/80% of the development costs.

- Producers must provide 20% from own funds.
- Producers are the only ones who can apply, but they must work together with a writer for the application.
- Local 'effect' required.
- Documentation includes: screenplay, budget, financing plan, bio-filmography, production declaration, shooting schedule or effect.

(2) Screenplays:

- Will grant DM 30 000 for a writer; maximum paid out is DM 60 000.
- No own funds requirement. Awarded as a grant – producers and the writer can apply.
- Documents to be submitted include: screenplay/project description, dialogue of a scene, bio-filmography, whether other subsidy has been applied for or received, copyright declaration, production declaration.

Filmbüro NRW e.V.
Leineweberstraße 1
45468 Mülheim an der Ruhr
Tel: +49 208 44 9841; Fax: +49 208 47 4113
Enquiries: Mike Wiedemann

Activities and details:

- Overall annual budget: approximately DM 3.5m.

(1) Project preparation:

- Awards of DM 30 000 (maximum given is DM 60 000).
- Own contribution by writer applicant of 10%.
- Awarded as grant, only writers can apply.
- Local 'effect' requirement.
- Must submit script/project description, bio-filmography, budget, financing plan, cast and crew.

(2) Screenplays:

- Awards of DM 30 000 (maximum given is DM 60 000).
- Own contribution by writer applicant of 10%.
- Awarded as grant, only writers can apply.
- Local 'effect' requirement.
- Must submit script/project description, bio-filmography, budget, financing plan, cast and crew.

Mecklenburg-Vorpommern-Film e.V.
Landesfilmzentrum
Röntgenstraße 22
19055 Schwerin
Tel: +49 385 55 50 77 80; Fax: +49 385 512 771

Enquiries: Gabriele Kotte

Activities and details:

- Total of DM 800 000 for fund's annual budget.

(1) Project and story development for feature films:

- A maximum of DM 30 000 awarded as grant to writer or filmmaker applicants.
- Must submit script/project description, treatment, budget, copyright declaration, notification of whether appplid and/or received subsidy from other fund.
- Local 'effect' requirement.

LOWER SAXONY
Filmförderung des NDR (Film fund by broadcaster NDR)
Niedersächsische Landestreuhandstelle für Wirtschaftsförderung, Bereich Filmförderung, Hamburger Allee 4, 30161 Hanover
Tel: +49 511 36 10; Fax: +49 511 361 5706
Enquiries: Frau Beyer

Activities and details:

- Total budget: approximately DM 4.5m

(1) Story and project development:

- Awards of DM 30 000 (maximum) as grants.
- Producers and writers can apply.
- Local 'effect' requirement.
- Must submit script/project description, bio-filmography, budget, financing plan.

(2) Scripts

- Awards of DM 30 000 (maximum) as grants.
- Producers and writers can apply.
- Local 'effect' requirement.
- Must submit script/project description, bio-filmography, budget, financing plan.

hr-Filmförderung

Schweizer Straße 6, 60594 Frankfurt am Main
Tel: +49 69 620 167; Fax: +49 69 603 21 85

Activities and details:

- Annual overall budget for project development, screenplay funding, production funding: DM 1m.
- Public broadcaster Hessischer Rundfunk set up this fund late last year as a complement to Hesse Film Fund.

(1) Project development

- Provides up to 20% (maximum), awarded as a grant.
- Only producers can apply.
- Regional 'effect' required.
- Must submit with application screenplay, budget, financing plan, bio-filmography, copyright declaration.

(2) Scripts

- Provides 20% as a grant, maximum can be 50%.
- Producers and writers can apply.
- Must submit with application screenplay, budget, financing plan, bio-filmography, copyright declaration.

Filmbüro Hessen
Schweizer Straße 6, 60594 Frankfurt, Germany
Tel: +49 69 62 01 67; Fax: +49 69 603 21 85
Enquiries: Jürgen Karg

Activities and details:

- Loans for script development of up to ECU 15 000.
- Limit is 80% of the total development costs.
- The plot must be connected with the state of Hessen.

Saarländisches Filmbüro e.V.
Nauwieserstraße 19, 66111 Saarbrücken, Germany
Tel: +49 6 81 360 47; Fax: +49 6 81 374 668
Enquiries: Christian Fuchs

Activities and details:

- Aid for script development.
- Loans of up to DM 30 000.
- Writers are the only ones eligible to apply, regional 'effect' requirement.
- Must submit script/project description, budget, copyright declaration, financing plan, scene of dialogue, notification of whether applied and/or received subsidy from other fund.
- Local 'effect' requirement.

(1) Project preparation:

- Loans of up to DM 30 000
- Writers are the only ones eligible to apply, regional 'effect' requirement.
- Must submit script/project description, budget, copyright declaration,

financing plan, scene of dialogue, notification of whether applied and/or received subsidy from other fund.
* Local 'effect' requirement.

Note: There is an agreement between the cultural film funds of Hessen, Saarland, Lower Saxony, NRW, Schleswig-Holstein and Mecklenburg Vorpommern that the regional 'effect' requirement can be waived (if a film receives backing from more than one of these funds.)

8.8   GREECE

Greek Film Centre
10 Panepistimiou Avenue, 10671 Athens, Greece
Tel: +30 1 363 4586; Fax: +30 1 361 4336
Enquiries: Ellie Petrides/Viola Georgakakau

Activities and details:

* The Centre tends to act as the primary producer of supported films.
* Its annual budget is around ECU 4m.
* Fourteen films supported in production in 1993.
* A new script department was set up in 1990, where treatments and scripts receive much higher attention than previously.
* Overheads are covered by the Centre.
* All support is for domestic language projects
* A separate fund is now available for writing and development, supporting the writing of the script to a first draft stage.
* If the writer/director is new, then the figure is around ECU 5000–7000.
* A percentage of this development sum is given to the producer/co-producer; this is decided by the GFC's council. Amounts vary.

8.9   ICELAND

Icelandic Film Fund
Lauavegi 24, 121 Reykjavik, Iceland
Tel: +354 1 623 580; Fax: +354 1 627 171
Enquiries: Mr B. Schram (Director)

Activities and details:

* Support for script development and pre-production.
* No support is repayable, it is a direct non-returnable grant.
* Grants vary in amount, with no strict rules over development support.

Films developed by the Icelandic Film Fund:
The Children of Nature

Movie-Days
The Sacred Mound

8.10 IRELAND

The Irish Film Board
The Halls, Quay Street, Galway, Ireland
Tel: +35 3 91 561398; Fax: +35 3 91 561405
Enquiries: Tracy Geraghty/James Flynn

Activities and details:

- Loans for project development, up to a maximum of ECU 33 000.
- Teams or individuals (producer/writer/director) can apply.
- Loans are repayable on the first day of production.
- Evidence of rights, where appropriate, should be submitted for application.
- Development budget and development schedule are also required.
- Application deadlines are January, May and September (for 1995).

Films funded by the Irish Film Board:
Broken Harvest
Words Upon the Window Pane
Ailsa
High Boot Benny
Moondance
A Man of No Importance
Guiltrip
Nothing Personal

8.11 ITALY

Premio Solinas
Via Di Monte, Testaccio, Rome 00153, Italy
Tel: +39 6 578 1079; Fax: +39 6 573 0068
Enquiries: Francesca Solinas

Activities and details

- A highly competitive screenplay writing award.
- Application details from the above address.

8.12 LUXEMBOURG

Fonds National du Soutien à la Production Audiovisuel (Luxembourg Film Fund)

c/o Ministère des Affaires Culturelles, 5 rue Zoufftgen, 3598 Dudelange, Luxembourg
Tel: +352 52 51 91 83
Enquiries: Jean Black

Activities and details:

- The Fund was created in 1990 and its annual budget is around ECU 2.2m.
- Designed to provide development and production support for feature films and television productions.
- Script writing support is in the form of non-repayable grants.
- Further development support is in the form of repayable loans.
- Of the 15 films awarded support in 1993, only two received script support. The rest received support for production and distribution and were given to short films and documentaries.

8.13   NORWAY

Ministry of Cultural Affairs
Postboks 8030, 0030 Oslo, Norway
Tel: +47 22 34 9090; Fax: +47 22 34 8039
Enquiries: Solvi Ollingsen (main point of contact for all other support funds in the country)

The Nordic Film and Television Fund
Nordic Film & TV Fund
Skovvejen 2, 0257 Oslo, Norway
Tel: +47 22 56 01 23; Fax: +47 22 56 12 23
Enquiries: Ivan Køhn

Activities and details:

- The aim is to support co-productions between Denmark, Sweden, Finland, Iceland and Norway.
- The fund concentrates on production and distribution support.
- Little development funding available other than in exceptional cases.

Det Norske Filminstitutt (The Norwegian Film Institute)
Postboks 482, Sentrum, 0105 Oslo, Norway
Tel: +47 22 42 87 40; Fax: +47 22 33 22 77

Activities and details:

- Script development loans available.

- Levels of awards vary.
- Application forms and details from above address.

Films developed by the Norwegian Film Institute:
Draumspel
Hudet Over Vannet
Over Stork De Stein
Legrafisten

Audiovisuelt Produksjonfond
c/o The Norwegian Film Institute
Postboks 482, Sentrum, 0105 Oslo, Norway
Tel: +47 22 42 87 40; Fax: +47 22 33 22 77

The Norwegian Centre for Film Screen Studies
8b Storengveien, 1342 Jar, Norway
Tel: +47 67 53 00 33; Fax: +47 67 12 48 65
Enquiries: Elin Erichsen (head of studies)

The Norwegian Cassette Duty Fund (aka: The National Compensation Fund for the Use of Recorded Sound and Images)
9, Ovre Volltate, 0158 Oslo, Norway
Tel: +47 22 33 52 50; Fax: +47 22 42 89 49

Norsk Film
PO Box 4, 1343 Jar, Norway
Tel: +47 67 52 53 00; Fax: +47 67 12 51 08
Enquiries: Harald Ohrvik (head of production)

8.14 PORTUGAL

Instituto Portugues de Artes Cinematograficas e Audiovisuais (IPACA) (Portuguese Film Institute)
Rua San Pedro de Alcantara 45, 1 Apt., 1200 Lisbon, Portugal
Tel: +351 1 346 84 85; Fax: +351 1 37 27 77
Enquiries: Salvato Telles De Meneses (vice president)

Activities and details:

- The only source of public finance for development in Portugal.
- Overall development budget of ECU 500 000.
- IPACA supports the development of six to eight projects a year.
- Payments are non-repayable grants, although this is under review.
- Script writing grants are worth from ECU 5000 to 7500.

8.15   SPAIN

Instituto de la Cinematografía y de las Artes Audiovisuales (ICAA)
(Spanish Film Institute)
Ministerio de Cultura, Plaza del Rey 1, 28004 Madrid, Spain
Tel: +34 1 532 50 89; Fax: +34 1 523 35 87 or 522 93 77
Enquiries: Beatriz de Armas

Activities and details:

(1) Aid for script creation

- Only writers can apply.
- Money is strictly grant money for writers and not subsidy funding for fully-fledged development and does not have to be repaid.
- The amount of the grant is variable, depending on the budget and the number of projects presented and approved.
- The aid is not compatible with any other type of national or foreign public-sector aid for the same script.

(2) Project-based subsidies for production of feature-length films

- Only producers can apply.
- The money operates as an advance for pre-production.
- A total ECU 4.6m budget has been set for 1995.
- Advance subsidies for feature films are limited to projects with relatively new directors attached who have made no more than two films previously.
- The funds will only be applied to low budget features.
- A maximum limit per film is set at 50% of the budget or ECU 1.2m, whichever is reached first.
- Projects with 'particularly difficult financial schemes' may benefit from support granted on an exceptional basis.
- Among other requisites, applications must include: evidence of ownership of rights to the script, film script, a complete budget and a detailed financing plan.
- All subsidies are repayable on a sliding scale of return at the box-office.

(3) Multiple-project awards

- In 1994 a new grant of incentive money for production companies was established.
- It provides varying monies to packages of three films.
- The monies are not strictly 'development' finance. The subsidy operates as an advance for pre-production.

Generalitat de Catalunya
Departament de Cultura, Palau March, Rambla de Santa Monica 8, 08002 Barcelona, Spain

Tel: +34 3 318 5004; Fax: +34 3 301 2234
Enquiries: Sr Pérez Giner

Activities and details

- In February 1995 new guidelines for support to Catalan film and TV makers were announced.
- A specific overall allocation of ECU 205 000 has been set aside for development funding.
- Applicants can be producers and writers.
- Applicants must be residents in Catalunya.
- They may apply for up to ECU 17 000 per project.

8.16   SWEDEN

The Swedish Film Institute
PO Box 27126, 102 52 Stockholm, Sweden
Tel: +46 8 665 1100; Fax: +46 8 666 3755
Enquiries: Peter Hald, Peter Lysander

Activities and details:

- The Institute implemented a new system in the Spring of 1993.
- Development loans for features can go up to ECU 5500.
- Pre-production loans can go up to ECU 25 000–30 000.
- Support is only granted to Swedish productions or films initiated by a Swedish production company and intended to be produced with a strong Swedish artistic involvement.
- Development support is to be repaid when the film goes into production.
- Most of the films developed to date are yet to reach production.

The Nordic Film and Television Fund
See section **8.13 Norway**

8.17   THE NETHERLANDS
Dutch Film Fund
Jan Luykenstraat 2, 1071 CM Amsterdam, The Netherlands
Tel: +31 20 664 3368; Fax: +31 20 675 0398
Enquiries: Ryclef Rienstra (Chief Executive)

Activities and details:

- Loans for project development.
- Only producers can apply.
- Production budget has to be executed on form provided by the Fund.
- Producer must provide and secure at least 20% of the development budget.

- The maximum amount loaned per script could be selectively increased from a pre-1994 level of Dfl 25 000 to approximately Dfl 100 000–150 000.
- Producers requesting higher support sums could be required to match the amount of investment.
- Projects submitted should (a) have a 'high audience' potential; (b) be 'artistically important' films; or (c) have the support of a major producer with a successful track record.
- Of the total development budget of the Fund, 20% could go to new and emerging scriptwriters but maximum amounts should be limited.
- The subsidy could be doubled if the writer manages to link with a producer who is willing to put up similar matching funds for development support.

8.18 UNITED KINGDOM
British Film Institute (BFI) Production
29 Rathbone Street, London W1P 1AG, UK
Tel: +44 171 636 5587; Fax: +44 171 580 9456
Enquiries: Helen Walker (Script Coordinator)

Activities and details:

- Development deals are nearly all director-led.
- No development money is available directly to producers.
- Established April 1994, although BFI Production has operated a development scheme since 1986.
- Although the emphasis is to launch new directors who are innovative and unusual, development finance is for the script.
- The total development budget of ECU 65 000 is divided into grants to five to seven projects per annum.
- Standard development deal is ECU 6500 for two drafts.
- The budget of the project must be below ECU 600 000.
- BFI considers this money an investment, not a loan, since they intend to produce the projects that they deliver.
- Apply any time of the year (500 submissions received annually).
- Repayment terms: if BFI goes on to produce the film, investment is written off or absorbed into the production budget. If script goes into turnaround, repayment is on first day of principal photography.

Films developed by BFI:
Madagascar Skin
Three Steps to Heaven

British Screen Finance Ltd
14–17 Wells Mews, 4th Floor, London W1P 3FL, UK

Tel: +44 171 323 9080; Fax: +44 171 323 0092
Enquiries and application: Stephen Cleary (head of development)

Activities and details:

(1) Screenplay loans

- Established 1991.
- Only writers can apply
- Loans to approximately 10–15 writers per year.
- Producers are normally not attached and are not required for the writer's application to be considered.
- Fixed loans of ECU 6500 to writers to get to first draft.
- Loans are interest-free and no repayment commission is charged.
- Repayment terms: on commencement of filming of the script or rolled over into further aid (see below).
- Apply any time during the year.

(2) Development loans

- Only producers can apply.
- Established in 1991.
- Loans to approximately 20 producers per year.
- Average amount spent on a developed project that goes into production is between ECU 65 000 and 90 000; a significant proportion is spent on script development.
- Loans are interest-bearing – rates vary – and are made to the production company.
- British Screen takes security for the loan in the form of a charge on the production company's assets.
- Apply any time during the year with a treatment, the project's history and the CVs of applicants.
- Repayment terms: full amount of loan is repayable on first day of principal photography, plus an additional figure of 50% of the British Screen loan, plus a percentage of net profit.

(3) Pre-production loans

- Established in 1991.
- Variable loans – on average ECU 12 800 – to finance final development of script, final
- Pre-production costs and to procure further finance for production.
- Loans are interest-bearing, with rates variable.
- Apply any time during the year, directly to Simon Perry or Stephen Cleary.
- Repayment terms: full amount of loan is repayable on the first day of principal photography, plus 50% of the loan and an additional negotiable percentage of net profit.

Films developed by British Screen Finance Ltd:

The Young Poisoner's Handbook
Rob Roy
Clockwork Mice
Love's Executioner
Orlando
Tom and Viv
Before the Rain
Land and Freedom

Scottish Film Production Fund (SFPF)
74 Victoria Crescent Road, Glasgow G12 9JN, UK
Tel: +44 41 337 2526; Fax: +44 41 337 2562
Enquiries: Eddie Dick (Director)/Ela Zych (Marketing and Promotions)

Activities and details:

- Only producers can apply for development awards.
- Established 1982.
- Up to ECU 19 000 loans for feature film script development.
- Repayment terms: the loan is repaid on the first day of principal photography, plus a flat-rate premium of 25% (e.g. an additional 25% of the original loan) repaid and up to 5% share of net profits when the film is completed.
- A board meets quarterly to consider applications.
- Apply initially to Eddie Dick well ahead of deadlines for formal submissions.
- Contact SFPF office for details.

Films developed by the SFPF:

Rob Roy
Shallow Grave
The Near Room
Easterhouse
Play Me Something
The Girl in the Picture

Appendix B:
Pan-European public funds for feature film development

European Script Fund (SCRIPT)
39c Highbury Place, London N5 1QP, UK
Tel: +44 171 226 9903; Fax: +44 171 54 2706
Enquiries: David Kavanagh (general director)/Christian Routh (selection coordinator)

Activities and details:

A pan-European Fund established in 1989 to stimulate the development of European fiction projects suitable for crossing European borders by providing conditionally repayable finance which has to be matched.

Note: SCRIPT officially stopped operating in June 1996, and a new MEDIA development agency will take the Fund's place. The following material is to demonstrate the range of schemes SCRIPT was operating through to the end of 1995.

The Fund operates five types of loans:

(1) Single writers

- SCRIPT is primarily producer-led, although it does provide about 60 loans for single writers (must not have a producer attached to the project) each year.
- Assessed on story potential.
- The maximum amount is customarily ECU 5000.
- The loan is released in two installments.
- A treatment and some dialogue is required to apply.

- Repayment conditions: loan is repayable on start of principal photography.

(2) Team loans

- Made to writers and producers working together.
- Assessed on story potential and production potential.
- SCRIPT makes 120–150 single project loans for film and TV fiction per annum.
- About three-quarters of SCRIPT funds go to developing movies.
- SCRIPT provides up to 50% of total development costs.
- Loans of up to maximum of ECU 37 500 may be granted.
- Loans are paid in three installments: (a) on signature of loan agreement, (b) on receipt of the script and (c) on delivery of a development package.
- SCRIPT loans cover contributions towards scripts, producer's overheads, producer's fee, budgeting, travel for research and to raise finance, option/rights fees, professional fees, translation costs, etc.
- SCRIPT can take 3 months to respond but a Fast Track operates if a producer gives a convincing reason why he needs an earlier decision.
- Producers can apply at any stage in the development of their project.
- Loans are interest-bearing.
- Repayment conditions: loan, plus 5%, on first day of principal photography.

(3) Second-stage funding

- Established in 1992 as an additional loan system aimed at enhancing an already funded project's potential.
- Producers can get top-up funding to move from completed script to pre-production.
- Amounts vary according to the project.
- Top-up funding is interest-bearing.
- Apply at any time.
- Repayment conditions: as per 'Teams' above.

(4) Incentive funding

- Established in 1991 as a multi-project loan scheme for production companies.
- Established producers can apply the development of usually three or more projects which may be drawn over a period of 1 year.
- Normal maximum: ECU 120 000 payable in a single installment.
- SCRIPT provides 30% of development costs.
- Repayment conditions: as per 'Teams' above.

(5) Incentive funding for television companies

- Established in 1994.
- Loans to independent production companies for the development of television drama projects.
- European broadcasters can apply.
- The TV companies allocate the loan funds to four (or more) projects.
- At least one of these projects must be a series and involve at least two different independent production companies.
- Normal maximum: ECU 200 000 payable according to an agreed cashflow per project.

Films developed by SCRIPT:

The Neon Bible
Rob Roy
Farinelli
Neak Sre
Orlando
Toto le Héros
Naked
The Cement Garden
The Young Americans
Daens
Jeanne la Pucelle

Appendix C: Pan-European training/development initiatives

ACE – Ateliers du Cinéma Européen (European Film Studio)
68 Rue de Rivoli, 75004 Paris, France
Tel: +33 1 4461 88 30; Fax: +33 1 4461 88 40
Enquiries: Colin Young (Director)/Claudie Cheval (Deputy Director)

Activities and details:

- Established in 1993 by the Media Business School and the Club of European Producers, ACE is an umbrella studio for the development of European feature films in a way to strengthen their chances of securing the widest possible audience.
- ACE does not provide development finance.
- ACE is aimed to European producers who already have some track record and have a project in active development, assisting them through the development process by providing expertise on script, finance and distribution.
- ACE selects approximately 10–12 producers for each contract period (two selections of participants in each calendar year).
- ACE enters into an agreement with each producer for an initial period of 6 months which is arranged to suit the schedules of the producers.
- In consultation with members of the ACE board, each project and its commercial prospects is closely analysed.
- Participating producers are brought together in Paris for an initial 5-day workshop to examine the international marketplace and distribution/marketing strategies, the primary emphasis being Europe.
- Each producer is assigned a 'godparent' – senior producers or other industry professionals chosen for their expertise and interest in a

particular project – who will oversee the project throughout its various development stages.

- ACE can also call upon a team of consultants, including script editors, financial experts, and sales, distribution and marketing executives to provide input to projects.
- Application procedure: producers should initially send a filmography, their CV and their company profile, having made first an inquiry through the central offices.
- Producers selected will pay a fee of ECU 5000.

Films currently in development with ACE:

Horse With No Name
The Lake
Dina's Book
Le Grand Meaulnes

EAVE (Les Entrepreneurs de l'Audiovisuel Européen)
14, Rue de la Presse, 1000 Brussels, Belgium
Tel: +32 2 219 0920; Fax: +32 2 223 0034
Enquires: Raymond Ravar (Managing Director)

Note: EAVE stopped operating at the end of 1995.

Activities and details:

- A producer's training initiative of the MEDIA Programme.
- Professional training services to European film and television producers.
- Producers with projects at the development stage are eligible for participation.
- Candidates with no specific projects can also participate.
- The programme extends over a 1-year period, and training is given at 8-day intensive workshops which are held three times during the year.
- The fee is approximately ECU 2000 for participants with projects and ECU 1000 for participants without project.
- Application forms can be obtained from the above EAVE offices.

Recent projects whose producers had gone through EAVE:
Rob Roy (producer: Peter Broughan)
Tales of a Hard City (producer: Alex Usborne)

Equinoxe
85–89, Quai Andre Citroën, 75711 Paris Cédex 15, France
Tel: +33 1 44 25 71 44; Fax: +33 1 44 25 71 42
Enquiries: Noëlle Deschamps (Vice-President)

Activities and details:

- A major training initiative for screenplay writers in association with the Sundance Institute.
- The aim of the workshops is to offer young European and American screenwriters the opportunity to perfect their scripts and to confront their ideas amongst established professionals on an international level.
- Open to young writers of all nationalities.
- The selected participants must have already some professional experience.
- They are required to present the final draft of their screenplay and to be able to speak either French or English fluently.
- The Equinoxe screenwriting workshops take place each year at the Château Beychevelle (France) in the Autumn and the Spring.
- For further details and interview with Noëlle Deschamps see Chapter 6.

First Film Foundation (FFF)
Canalot Production Studios, 222 Kensal Road, London W10 5BN, UK
Tel: +44 181 969 5195; Fax: +44 181 960 6302
Enquiries: Angeli MacFarlane/Ivan McTaggart

Activities and details:

- Established in 1989.
- Does not provide development finance.
- Does provide facilities to feature film and television writers, producers and directors who are starting out in the industry, primarily in the UK.
- Facilities include script reading, legal advice, accounting and administrative services, travel costs, and introduction to professionals.
- Apply any time during the year by sending a script.

Films developed by the FFF:

Leon the Pig Farmer
Soft Top Hard Shoulder
Flight of the Innocent
Paler than Grass
Feeney's Rainbow
Petards d'Amour (France)
Fallen Angels

PILOTS (Programme for the International Launch of Television Series)
Diputació 279–283, 08007 Barcelona, Spain
Tel: +34 3 488 1038; Fax: +34 3 487 4192
Enquiries: Thomas Spieker

Activities and details:

- A workshop/training format for the development of long-running television series.
- A programme to improve the quality of long-running series produced in Europe, raising standards of script writing and increasing the ability of European series to reach larger audiences and 'cross borders'.
- Aimed at broadcasters and/or independent producers with a long-running series project and a writing team (a script editor and the producer, and one or more writers)
- Great emphasis is placed on the role of the script editor.
- Participating teams work together for a period of 5 months; two workshops are held, with a period between them for rewriting under supervision of the course tutors and experts.
- The key learning techniques include didactic (lectures, seminars, analysis of drama series episodes); reading and analysing each other's work, and the actual rewriting of their pilot scripts by participants under supervision of the course tutors.

Series developed by PILOTS:
Ballymoy (Warner Sisters/Parallel Films)
Greek Idyll (Saskia Sutton/Blossom Productions)
Poble Nou (TV3 Telelisio de Catalunya)

The Frank Daniel Script Workshops
c/o Metropolis Film, Bergmannstraße 91, 10961 Berlin, Germany
Tel: +49 30 693 2326; Fax: +49 30 693 4648
Enquiries: Rose-Marie Couture

Activities and details:

- A course designed by scriptwriter and pedagogue Frank Daniel, organized by Metropolis Film and supported by Filmboard Berlin-Brandenburg.
- For scriptwriters, producers and commissioning editors with a script, a treatment or a new idea.
- The workshops have four complementary sections for participants in various phases of the writing process, including scene writing and story structure, treatment for a feature-length screenplay, feature scripts and producer's Master Class.
- All discussions are carried out in English in the workshop groups and film analysis.
- Cost per workshop (the four sections): ECU 1400.

Appendix D: The large and medium-sized private companies in Europe

Babelsberg Film & Fernsehproduktion Gmbh
August Bebel Straße, 26–53, 14482 Postdam, Germany
Tel: +49 331 721 2006; Fax: +49 331 721 2053
Contact: Reinhard Klooss/Ingrid Windisch

Canal Plus
85–89, Quai André Citröen, 75711 Paris Cedex 15, France
Tel: +33 1 44 25 10 00; Fax: +33 1 44 25 12 34
Contact: Caroline Ryan

CiBy 2000
90, Avenue des Champs Elysees, 75008 Paris, France
Tel: +33 1 44 21 64 00; Fax: +33 1 44 20 64 48
Contact: Jean François Fonlupt

CiBy Sales
10 Stephen Mews, London W1P 1PP, UK
Tel: +44 171 333 8877; Fax: +44 171 333 8878
Contact: Tom Strudwick

CINEVOX
Bavariafilmplatz 7, 82031 Geiselgasteig, Munich, Germany
Tel: +49 89 649 2604; Fax: +49 89 649 3288
Contact: Dieter Geissler

Chargeurs
5, Blv. Malesherbes, 75008 Paris, France
Tel: +33 1 49 24 43 42; Fax: +33 1 49 24 43 50
Contact: Timothy Burrill (see Guild Film Distribution below)

Chrysalis Films
The Chrysalis Building, 13, Bramley Road, London W10 6SP, UK
Tel: +44 171 221 2213; Fax: +44 171 221 6455/229 1521
Contact: Lyndsay Posner

Enigma Productions Ltd
Pinewood Studios, Iver Heath, Buckinghamshire SL0 0NH, UK
Tel: +44 753 630 555; Fax: +44 753 630 393
Contact: David Puttnam/Steve Norris

Filmauro Srl
Via della Vasca Navale, 58, 00187 Rome, Italy
Tel: +39 6 556 07 88; Fax: +39 6 559 06 70
Contact: Luciano Grisant/Rita Poggi

Gaumont
30, Ave. Charles de Gaulle, 92200 Neuilly-sur-Seine, France
Tel: +33 1 46 43 20 00; Fax: +33 1 46 43 21 68
Contact: Patrice Ledoux/Sidonie Seydoux

Guild Film Distribution Ltd
Kent House, 14–17 Market Place, Great Titchfield Street, London W1N 8AR,
UK
Tel: +44 171 323 5151; Fax: +44 171 631 3568
Contact: Timothy Burrill

Hachette Premiere
10, rue de Marignan, 75008 Paris, France
Tel: +33 1 42 25 19 70; Fax: +33 1 42 56 00 81
Contact: René Cleitman

Neue Constantin Filmproduktion GmbH
Kaiserstraße 39, 80801 München, Germany
Tel: +49 89 386090; Fax: +49 89 3860 9242
Contact: Herman Weigel

Nordisk Film & TV A/S
Mosedalsvej, 2500 Valby, Denmark
Tel: +45 36 30 10 33; Fax: +45 31 16 85 02
Contact: Lars Kolvig/Hans Morten Rubin

Polygram Filmed Entertainment
8, St James Square, London SW1Y 4JU, UK
Tel: +44 171 747 4000; Fax: +44 171 747 4499
Contact: Stewart Till/Michael Kuhn

RCS Produzione TV SpA
Viale Liegi 41, 00198 Rome, Italy
Tel: +39 6 855 52 000; Fax: +39 6 855 53 13
Contact: Mario di Francesco

Sogetel SA
Gran Via, 32 – 1°, 28013 Madrid, Spain
Tel: +34 1 521 7405; Fax: +34 1 523 2366
Contact: Fernando de Garcillán

UFA
Fernsehproduktion GmbH
Kleiststraße 23–26, 10787 Berlin, Germany
Tel: +49 30 21 00 070; Fax: +49 30 21 00 07 49
Contact: Wolf Bauer/Axel Reick/Norbert Sauer

UGC International
24, Ave. Charles de Gaulle, 92522 Neully-sur-Seine, France
Tel: +33 1 46 40 44 00; Fax: +33 1 47 22 05 12
Contact: Alain Sussfield

Working Title Films Ltd
Oxford House, 76 Oxford Street, London W1N 9FD, UK
Tel: +44 171 307 3000; Fax: +44 171 307 3001/2/3
Contact: Deborah Hayward

Appendix E: European-based literary/talent agencies

Artmedia
10, Ave. Georges Cinq, Paris 75008, France
Tel: +33 1 44 31 22 00; Fax: +33 1 47 20 02 52
Contact: Francois-Xavier Molin

Alexandra Cann Representatives
337 Fulham Road, London SW10 9TW, UK
Tel: +44 171 352 6266; Fax: +44 171 352 2294
Contact: Alexandra Cann

AP Watt
20 John Street, London WC1N 2DR, UK
Tel: +44 171 405 6774; Fax: +44 171 831 2154
Contact: Rod Hall/Nick Marston

Blake Friedmann
37–41 Gower Street, London WC1E 6HH, UK
Tel: +44 171 631 4331; Fax: +44 171 323 1274
Contact: Julian Friedmann

Casarotto Company
National House, 60–66 Wardour Street, London W1V 3HP, UK
Tel: +44 171 287 4450; Fax: +44 171 287 9128
Contacts: Jenne Casarotto/Greg Hunt

Curtis-Brown
162–168 Regent Street, London W1R 5TB, UK
Tel: +44 171 872 0331; Fax: +44 171 872 0332
Contact: Leah Schmidt

ICM (UK)
Oxford House, 76 Oxford Street, London W1R 8AX, UK
Tel: +44 171 636 6565; Fax: +44 171 323 0101
Contact: Duncan Heath/Michael Foster/Sue Rodgers

International Media Consulting
Goethestraße 17, 80336 Munich, Germany
Tel: +49 89 581 0238; Fax: +49 89 550 3855
Contact: Sigrid Narjes

Peters, Fraser & Dunlop
503/4 The Chambers, Chelsea Harbour, London SW10 0XF, UK
Tel: +44 171 376 7676; Fax: +44 171 352 7356
Contact: Anthony Jones/Tim Corrie/Norman North/Gavin Knight

Rochelle Stevens & Company
2 Terrets Place, Upper Street, London N1 1QZ, UK
Tel: +44 171 359 3900; Fax: +44 171 354 5729
Contact: Rochelle Stevens

William Morris Agency (UK)
31–32 Soho Square, London W1V 5DG, UK
Tel: +44 171 434 2191; Fax: +44 171 434 0238
Contact: Steve Kenis/Philip Adler/Ben Silverman

Index